Global Goals for S[ ]
Transformation

Volume IV: Driving Businesses Towards the SDGs

Seema Goyal

walnutpublication
.com

INDIA • UK • USA

Paperback ISBN: 979-8-89171-218-8
eBook ISBN: 979-8-89171-219-5

This book has been published following reasonable efforts to ensure the material is free from errors, with the author's full consent.
The publisher does not endorse or guarantee the accuracy, reliability, or completeness of the Content and expressly disclaims any liability for errors or omissions. No warranties of any kind are made, whether express or implied, including but not limited to warranties of merchantability or fitness for a particular purpose, or that the Content constitutes educational or medical advice.

First Published in May, 2025

Published by Walnut Publication

(an imprint of Vyusta Platforms Private Limited)

www.walnutpublication.com

India

Unit# 909, 9th Floor, Wave Silver Tower, Sector-18, Noida - 201301

UK

71-75 Shelton Street, Covent Garden, London, WC2H 9JQ, UK

Distributed by

🏛 ZopioTail

This Book is Dedicated to All of You

Acknowledgment

This book is the product of countless conversations, collaborations, and collective insights — and it would not have been possible without the support of many individuals and institutions.

First and foremost, I express my deepest gratitude to all the educators, researchers, and policy leaders whose dedication to sustainable development and social equity continues to inspire this work. Your vision, scholarship, and perseverance laid the foundation for this inquiry.

Thank you for your guidance, your patience, and your unwavering belief in this project. Your insights challenged me to think more deeply and write more clearly.

To the communities, organizations, and field practitioners who generously shared their experiences and time — your stories gave this book its purpose and direction.

To my family and friends, thank you for your encouragement, emotional strength, and the many quiet sacrifices that allowed this work to take shape.

Our many thanks to every reader and changemaker committed to turning Global goals into local action. It is our hope that this work serves not just as a reference, but as a catalyst for continued dialogue, innovation, and transformation.

Finally, I acknowledge the many unsung contributors across sectors — educators in classrooms, students in discussion, policy advocates in negotiation rooms — who work daily to bring the Sustainable Development Goals from vision to reality.

About the Author

Educationist| SDG Advocate | Interdisciplinary Researcher | Sustainability Consultant | Founder of SDG Readiness Platform.

Seema Goyal, an Interdisciplinary researcher on SDGs in terms of Education, business and policy making, eager to reimagine the future as a more socially and environmentally just world, committed towards achieving the SDGs. With 20+ years-experience in curriculum design and assess Education sector policies, strategies and programs with a view of ensuring comparability to International best practices, smart solutions and technological advances, and responsiveness to development needs of the country.

We see the purpose of SDG Readiness Platform, as being a catalyst for change that will have an impact. It is a Platform working on SDG's and Climate crisis and aims to leave behind a legacy to inspire people and various stakeholders in this arena about solutions.

Our mission is to get the leaders to meet and learn from each other and be inspired by each other. We want to get this awareness out to millions. This is more than a book, a series of pro-planet book written for everyone –wherever you might be in the world. It is for those who want to easily understand how Climate Change is affecting the planet and who want to make small, simple changes in their everyday lives to become climate aware.

By sharing knowledge, leading by example, and creating spaces for conversation, I've found that I can engage others in meaningful discussions about sustainability. It's a journey that doesn't just involve personal commitment but also empowering others to understand how their actions, whether big or small, can contribute to a more sustainable world.

Gandhi told us to 'be the change we want to see in the world.' This book captures that spirit, reminding us that everyone can do something to help the planet."

Seema Goyal

Preface

Dangers of the Growth Imperative - Degrowth A More Scientific Approach to Economics

The climate emergency, rising inequalities and the COVID-19 pandemic have reaffirmed the failures and limitations of the current neoliberal model to respond to crises and ensure a dignified life for all. Transformation in the organization of our economy is needed in order to confront the challenges the world is currently facing and to create societies that are fair, inclusive, socially-just, equitable and sustainable.

We are at a critical juncture. At a time when the world faces a series of crises, from the environmental emergency to hunger and deepening inequalities, increasing armed conflicts, pandemics, rising extremism, and escalating inflation, a collective response is growing. A large movement is building and concrete solutions are emerging to counter the dominant paradigm of growth, privatization and commodification.

Reliance on mathematical models and statistical analysis has led economics to become too focused on technical details and has lost sight of the broader social and political implications of economics. Factors that cannot be quantified or easily modeled, such as cultural and historical context, power dynamics, and environmental and ethical considerations, are left out entirely when policies are made solely on the basis of statistical models and their predictions.

The pursuit of economic growth has become the universal goal of public policy and economic decision-making, increasing overall prosperity and improving living standards. However, this focus on growth has also led to the over-exploitation of resources and humans and destroyed the environment.

One way the growth narrative has contributed to the over-exploitation of resources is by promoting the extraction and consumption of natural resources faster than they can be replenished. This has led to environmental degradation and the depletion of natural resources.

In addition, the pursuit of economic growth has also been criticized for leading to the exploitation of human labor. Some have argued that the focus on growth has led to the creation of low-paying jobs, poor working conditions, and a lack of protections for workers.

The Business-as-Usual Scenario

The 30 Years findings were published in the book, Limits to Growth, stating that "if the present growth trends in world population, industrialization, pollution, food production, and resource depletion continue unchanged, the limits to growth on this planet will be reached sometime within the next one hundred years. The most probable result will be a rather sudden and uncontrollable decline in both population and industrial capacity." Recently Yale reported that the current empirical data is broadly consistent with the 1972 projections.

Given that natural resources are exhaustible, human activity, in the long run, will have to "decrease" to a scale that can be supported by solar energy.

This trend of scientists seeing through the cracks of the economy and realizing degrowth is the answer, continues in the 20th century. In 2018, over 200 scientists wrote to the EU institutions, insisting they explore possibilities for a post-growth future.

They demanded that they focus on well-being instead of growth, use better indicators to indicate progress than GDP, and actively discuss the economic transition. Perhaps, degrowth is nothing but a more scientific way to approach the question of how the world should function, ensuring well-being for all living and non-living things. As Federico Demaria puts it, degrowth challenges the hegemony of growth and calls for a democratically led redistributive downscaling of production and consumption to achieve environmental sustainability, social justice, and well-being for all. A radical transformation of our economies is the only way to save nature, and ourselves.

Earth Overshoot Day arrives earlier every year, showing we consume more resources than the planet can regenerate.

Meanwhile, 1% of the population controls nearly half of Global wealth, while millions remain in poverty. These are not minor issues. They are urgent signals: the system requires change.

A regenerative model of capitalism provides a clear solution by restoring resources instead of depleting them. For example, Patagonia promotes repairs and resale to minimize waste, while Danone invests in regenerative agriculture to support healthier ecosystems. Additionally, ESG investments have reached $40 trillion, showing that markets are increasingly adopting this approach.

By 2040, companies will no longer measure success solely by profits but by contributing to restoring the planet, redistributing wealth, and creating fairer systems. The opportunity is clear: regeneration drives the next stage of growth.

Contents

Chapter 3

Chapter 4

Chapter 1

Degrowth - Our Current Model of Capitalism is Breaking Capitalism and Climate Change - Moving towards Solutions

What is wrong with GDP?	What do alternatives need to capture?	What does this mean from each of these perspectives:				Existing /proposed Indicators, frameworks and examples
		Just	Feminist	Decolonial	Environmental	
Only covers part of the economy	Entire economy	All production	Production and reproduction	Formal and Informal	Benefits from envt'l goods and services respecting planetary boundaries	•Time-use •Ecological services
Does not show who benefits from growth	How economic activity is benefiting all	Economic wealth inequality	Intersectional inequality	Changes in inequality between Global North/South and between racialised groups	Equal access to natural resources	•Palma ratio •Multi-dimensional and intersectional approaches
Ignores how growth happens: quality or conditions, contribution to/detraction from social prosperity	Quality/ net impacts of economic activity	Decent work	Dignified work; freedom from harassment, time & income poverty	Global trade rules, net financial (including tax) and resource flows	Envt'l quality and resource stock, biodiversity & envt'l degradation	•Per capita carbon footprint •Cumulative carbon emissions •Time Poverty •Median wage x employment rate •Wellbeing Elsewhere •Loss & Damage Elsewhere
Does not capture social prosperity	Social prosperity	Freedom from hunger & poverty	Safety, voice, time, sexual & reproductive rights; freedom from violence	Reciprocity, justice & solidarity		•Cost & availability of nutritious diet •Subjective wellbeing •Violence against women •Life expectancy •Community relationships
Single indicator, based on Eurocentric values and created/imposed by a group of rich countries	Dashboard of key multi-dimensional indicators, reflecting indigenous values. Developed and maintained through a bottom-up process	Inclusive process, centring indigenous voices and knowledge systems, prioritizing inclusion of women				•Community assemblies

New thinking on how we might leverage some of the powerful elements of capitalism to rein in greenhouse gas emissions this decade while we build the moral, equitable, sustainable economic business model of the future are -

1. Growth for growth's sake is incompatible with a thriving planet. At the same time, the principle of growth can be

1

harnessed to advance climate solutions — if deployed strategically.

2. Capitalism as currently practiced cannot continue indefinitely if we are to halt Climate Change. Some business models and sectors will need to pivot, and some will need to be phased out altogether.

3. That said, we can't wait for wholesale systems change. As the larger transformation gets underway, we can direct the capabilities and resources of corporations to implementing climate solutions quickly, safely, and equitably. And shareholders and employees can pursue opportunities to catalyze change within their own spheres of influence.

4. We need to see ourselves as different operators deploying different tactics, but all part of one larger team. Some of us work inside the system, changing it from within, and others push it faster from the outside, toward a shared North Star: a thriving, just, equitable world for eons to come.

5. "We're not talking about growth for growth's sake, let me be clear. We're talking about growth in hyper-strategic areas, laser-focused on climate solutions, and laser-focused on systematically replacing business as usual."

Global growth is slowing. The IMF just predicted below-average growth for this year and next. And yet, we still pretend this is a temporary dip rather than the reality of hitting planetary boundaries.

In 2015, the UN quietly stated what many still refuse to admit: Degrowth is our only option.

"Once in overshoot, the sustainable carrying capacity of the planet can only be re-established in one way: Down. Either through managed decline or through collapse—leaving it to the market or nature to reduce human activity."

The truth is, our choice isn't whether to keep growing or not—it's whether the end of growth happens by design or disaster.

Do we set our own limits and take care of what we still have?

Or do we push forward blindly until ecosystem breakdown forces those limits upon us?

This is not a doomsday prediction—it's a call to something better.

What comes next isn't just about survival; it's about Building a **Future Worth Arriving In - A future based on:**

A degrowth economy, where societies prioritize human and ecological wellbeing over profit and expansion—redistributing resources instead of hoarding them.

A world beyond exploitation, where the Global South is no longer forced to subsidize the overconsumption of the rich, and environmental and social justice reinforce each other instead of being pitted against one another.

An economy of reciprocity, where we produce and consume less but live better—meeting our physical, emotional, and spiritual needs through community, fairness, and sufficiency rather than accumulation.

Growth is not the goal. Justice is. And the sooner we embrace this, the more we all have to gain.

Business as usual won't cut it, even though we made progress before. Going back to pre-pandemic ways is not enough. We need a new paradigm built on the pillars of our 17 Global goals. Rethink conventions, flip the orthodoxies, governments, organizations, corporations, citizens of the world snap out of it, it's time for bold climate action, to act for women and girls, for social justice and inclusion. Scale up the transition to renewable energy. Create 85 million green jobs. Phase out fossil fuel subsidies and tax carbon. 2.8 trillion dollars. Keep your promises.

Support developing nations. Write off debts. Free up one trillion dollars for climate resilience, people and communities. 500 billion dollars for Africa to achieve universal energy access by 2030. Commit to a circular economy now. New resilient food systems - they can cut waste by 17 percent. Strengthen domestic financial institutions. Make insurance and banking accessible to everyone. Scale up the digital transformation to educate the 1.6 billion kids who missed school in the pandemic. Educate girls, including the 130 million not in school now. Ensure women's equal share of decision making. Eliminate discrimination against female workers and boost productivity by 40 percent.

Governments, companies and individuals have to come together to address the urgent climate crisis. Policymakers, business leaders and the Global workforce have a shared opportunity and responsibility.

Achieving our climate targets is a monumental task and it is going to take a whole-of-economy effort to make it happen. That means we need a transformation in the skills and jobs people have if we're going to get there.

Green skills are the core of the green transition and harnessing the shift of talent. Through a targeted approach, we can progressively shift towards these greener jobs, using skills to identify jobs with the highest ability to turn sectors and countries green. We need more opportunities for those with green skills, we have to upskill workers who currently lack those skills, and we need to ensure green skills are hardwired.

We cannot afford to leave anyone behind. We have a to-do list. We have the resources. Five years to reach our goals. We're on this planet together, so let's work together. Let's get the list done.

"With the geopolitical landscape shifting, we must sharpen our message on the inextricable ties between climate, nature and business, aligned with the triple bottom line to work for the benefit of people, planet and profit.

What is Sustainable Business

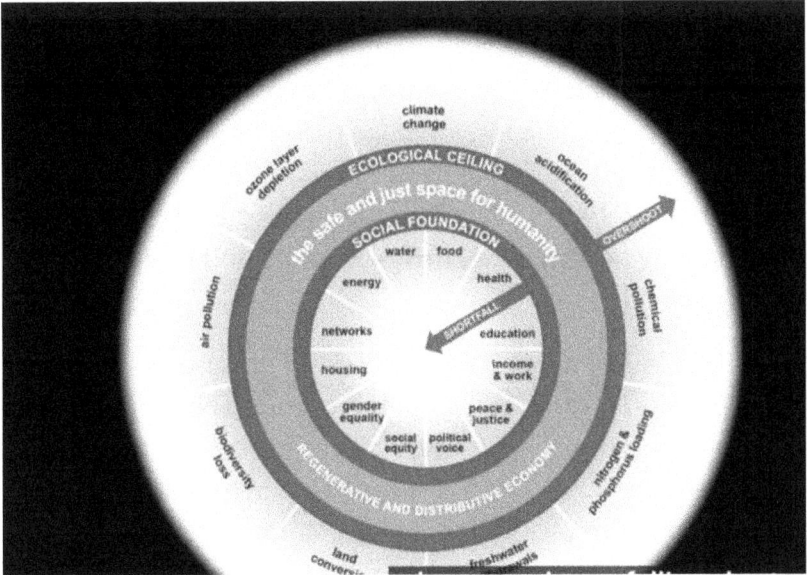

In our fast-paced world, economic policies play a crucial role in shaping our environment. Although the primary goal of these policies is to foster economic growth, their environmental impacts cannot be overlooked. Understanding this interaction is the first step towards more sustainable and equitable solutions.

Nature is a Human Right

Fighting for a green world — for building an equal, **healthier society**. Access to the natural world is a human right. This inspiring book captures why contact with nature is essential for our mental, social and physical well-being — and how we can rethink urban development to create green city spaces and a return to nature.

Environmental challenges, including Climate Change, are changing the way businesses work, either because they are forced to or because they proactively seek to. Green businesses are more profitable and future proof. They save scarce resources, help maintain healthy ecosystems, minimize pollution and waste, limit greenhouse emissions, and provide green goods and services that enable more responsible consumption patterns. Green businesses are vital for a development model that delivers a triple bottom-line of prosperity, planet and people. However, sustainability as a business driver is novel, and companies will need support in the process.

Therefore, business service providers are to support companies in the process towards greening the economy. The benefits from flourishing green businesses are twofold. The business community becomes more competitive while at the same time the jobs produced are supporting a societal change towards greener and healthier lives for people. Therefore, governments and private sector support agencies have a clear role and motive to promote greening of businesses and create an enabling environment for green business and job growth. Developed and middle-income countries are leading the way in supporting green business development, while a number of low-income countries are also taking positive steps. How do they do this? What works and what does not work in supporting green business development?

Valuing Nature Guide for Businesses

Nature is the foundation of human existence. Although businesses depend on nature for all activities, they undervalue and neglect it as an asset, leading to poor business decisions with respect to the natural world. Businesses face severe risks from nature loss, including lost biodiversity. A lack of action could result in soaring commodity prices, job losses, increased regulatory requirements, political instability and failure to achieve net-zero targets. By recognizing the need to value and protect nature as core to business purpose, board members can help create greater value for all stakeholders, while reinforcing their organization's physical and commercial resilience. Explore these risks and opportunities and outline key steps to help incorporate nature as core to business strategy.

Nature is the operating system of our planet, the foundation of human existence. All economic output stems from mother nature. Despite this reliance, business has historically undervalued and overlooked nature. Nature loss is already impacting business and the risks are increasing. We have a window of opportunity before us to stop and reverse the degradation of nature.

The Importance of Environmental Policies

From the bustling streets of New York to the serene villages in India, governments are adopting stringent environmental policies to tackle urgent challenges such as Climate Change, air pollution, and biodiversity loss. These policies aim to reduce emissions, enhance sustainability, and protect our natural resources. But the question remains: how do these policies affect our economies?

Economic Impacts of Environmental Policies: Challenges and Opportunities

Research shows that environmental policies, despite their costs to businesses, have a small overall impact on the economy. Stringent regulations may require investments in pollution control technologies, increasing production costs. However, the benefits, such as reduced healthcare expenses and improved worker productivity, often compensate for these costs.

Environmental policies create winners and losers across different sectors. High-polluting industries may face challenges, while more productive companies and cleaner sectors benefit from a healthier environment and new opportunities. For example, the renewable energy sector has seen tremendous growth due to supportive policies, creating new jobs and spurring innovation.

Balancing Economic and Environmental Goals: Innovative Strategies

Achieving a balance between economic growth and environmental protection requires innovative and integrated policies. Effective strategies include:

> **Incentives for Sustainable Practices:** Financial incentives can encourage companies to innovate and reduce their environmental impact.

- ➢ **Polluter Pays Principle:** Encouraging responsible behavior and reducing pollution by making polluters bear the costs of their environmental impact.

- ➢ **Investment in Green Technologies:** Supporting research and development in green technologies to drive innovation and create new economic opportunities while minimizing environmental harm.

- ➢ **Inclusive Policy Design:** Ensuring that environmental policies address the needs of vulnerable communities and promote social justice, enhancing their effectiveness and public support.

Strategy for SDG Progress

Faced with the alarming realities of Climate Change, companies are finally acknowledging the inevitable and incorporating ways of adapting to climate-driven disasters and disruptions into their business strategies, writes Trellis co-founder Joel Makower. They are assessing the physical risks to their operations and seeking to be ready, resourceful and resilient in the face of more frequent climate-borne disruptions.

How to reimagine our economies in respect of the planet's ecological limits Reviewing just transition and sustainability initiatives across the globe, including key measurement frameworks and the nexus between a just transition and the Sustainable Development Goals (SDGs)

A recent framework for company action published by PwC articulated the business case for adaptation: avoiding economic losses, protecting communities and ecosystems, and "increasing revenue, cost savings and sustainability."

Here are ways that companies can prepare and adapt:

- **Manage Risks:** Assess which aspects of the business are most susceptible to climate disruptions, and develop scenarios to understand potential impacts.

- **Adjust Operations:** Invest in energy-efficient technologies and renewable energy sources to reduce dependency on fossil fuels and stabilize costs.

- **Adapt Supply Chains:** Work with suppliers to improve their resilience to climate impacts, ensuring continuity of supply.

- **Monitor and Report Risks:** Include adaptation efforts in sustainability and annual reports to communicate progress and commitment to stakeholders.

- **Provide Leadership and Governance:** Ensure that adaptation approaches are regularly reviewed at the highest levels, and create teams to integrate them into all aspects of business operations and strategy.

- **Better Metrics for Economic Progress:** Governments are already looking into different metrics of development - and we must go beyond the "development as catching-up paradigm". Shared examples of how metrics are used in practice for big decisions taken in the various countries. What is missing is a better Global coordination - which could come from an Intergovernmental Panel on Wellbeing, Inclusion, Sustainability and the Economy, to among other things adopt a better progress indicator than GDP. Stakeholders have stressed the need for better metrics of progress.

- **A High Ambition Coalition for Wellbeing Economies:** Any Coalition should engage with feminist principles as well as learn from and collaborate with indigenous people and local communities, which hold much of the knowledge required to build Wellbeing Economies, living in close relationship, respect and balance with the land.

- **Redefining Prosperity and Enshrining Wellbeing in National Legislation:** National Governments and policymakers should enshrine the rights of future generations (social and environmental justice) in policymaking. support institutions in the application of the legislation, and monitor and assess the extent to which wellbeing objectives set by public bodies, instead of GDP growth, are being met. This means long term goals are not just policy aspirations but are enshrined in law, with institutions required to meet them.

- **Taking Immediate Action:** CFOs should Prioritize Practical sustainability Measures Instead of waiting for 2050 net-zero goals, CFOs can prioritise near-term, high-impact sustainability measures that generate measurable financial and environmental returns. The top investment priorities for 2025 can include:

  - **Sustainable Materials** – Reducing emissions by shifting to renewable and low-impact resources.

  - **Sustainable Innovation & Partnerships** – Investing in clean technology and collaborations that drive green solutions.

  - **Energy Management & Waste Reduction** – Lowering costs through energy efficiency and resource optimization.

- **Supply Chain Decarbonization** – Integrating sustainability into sourcing and logistics operations.

This shift also reflects a broader trend in corporate strategy — where financial leaders are moving from passive climate commitments to active, data-driven decision-making that integrates sustainability into core business functions.

Hard truths for Business Sustainability as We Go into 2025.

1. Climate Change is no longer a distant threat but an immediate strategic risk. Organisations must develop robust and forward-looking risk management frameworks that anticipate and mitigate potential disruptions.

2. Sustainability is not a cost center but an important source of innovation, operational efficiency, and competitive advantage. The most successful enterprises will view ecological constraints as catalysts for breakthrough strategies.

3. Global supply chains must be redesigned with transparency, circularity, and adaptability as core principles. Resilience now trumps pure cost optimisation.

4. Emerging technologies in artificial intelligence and robotics are critical enablers of sustainable transformation. They provide unprecedented capabilities for improving environmental performance.

5. The most competitive organisations will cultivate a workforce that views sustainability as an intrinsic professional competency, not a specialised function.

6. Anticipate increasingly stringent environmental regulations. Proactive compliance is no longer sufficient. Industry leadership requires setting new standards of corporate environmental stewardship.

7. Transparency is the new currency of brand loyalty. Consumers demand verifiable, substantive evidence of sustainability commitments, not superficial marketing narratives.

8. Sustainability challenges cannot be addressed through siloed approaches. Cross-sector collaboration, systems thinking, and holistic problem-solving are essential.

9. Recognise that organisational strategy must operate within scientifically defined planetary ecological boundaries.

10. The Biggest Challenge in Corporate Governance and Leadership for Environmental Sustainability involves -

Corporate sustainability, biodiversity and Climate Change transformation strategies, Circular and Regenerative business practices and nature-based solutions.

Understanding the "Why"

One of the most significant challenges in sustainability today is that many professionals, stakeholders, CEOs, and employees don't truly understand the "why" behind sustainability. This lack of understanding often leads to confusion, with sustainability being mistaken for environmental initiatives or social events alone. But sustainability is much more than that—it's about balancing the 3Ps: People, Planet, and Profit. It's about integrating sustainability into the mindset, the business strategy, and every employee in every department.

Understanding the "why" behind a company's sustainability actions is crucial because sustainability isn't just the responsibility of one department or a single leader — it must be embedded into every aspect of the business. This integration often requires existing roles to take on new sustainability-related responsibilities. However, if the "why" behind these responsibilities isn't clearly communicated, employees can quickly become overwhelmed and exhausted.

But is understanding the "why" enough? Not entirely. While knowing the "why" can motivate individuals and emphasize the significance of their new roles, it alone isn't sufficient. Employees also need adequate support to navigate these changes. Moreover, leveraging the existing knowledge and expertise within each department (whether in finance, sourcing, or operations) is essential to effectively integrate sustainability across the organization.

It's a mixture of educating existing employees on sustainability tasks, fostering an environment where you can maximize the expertise of current staff, and bringing in new talent with a passion for sustainability. By balancing these elements, organizations can truly embed sustainability into their core operations and achieve meaningful progress.

Explaining the "Why" does three Critical Things:

1. **Motivation:** It encourages individuals to see sustainability as a rewarding path, offering purpose and fulfillment in their roles.

2. **Perspective:** It highlights the vast opportunities and future possibilities within the sustainability sphere.

3. **Business Continuity:** It underscores how crucial sustainability is to business continuity, making it clear that it's part of everyone's job to ensure the company operates in the right way.

So why is this Understanding so Crucial?

1. **Critical Times:** We're facing unprecedented challenges — from Climate Change to biodiversity loss and deforestation, not to mention social injustices. These issues are interlinked and require a comprehensive approach to sustainability.

2. **Regulatory Landscape:** The regulatory environment is rapidly evolving, and businesses that don't keep up risk facing fines, reputational damage, and lost opportunities.

3. **Investment Attraction:** ESG (Environmental, Social, and Governance) performance is now a key indicator for investors. Platforms like eToro highlight how mainstream this has become — attracting investment means performing well in sustainability.

4. **Competitiveness:** Companies excelling in sustainability are setting the standard, and to stay competitive, others must step up. Customers are increasingly demanding sustainable practices, and businesses must meet these expectations.

5. **Operational Optimization:** Where sustainability meets profitability.

6. **Risk Management:** Effective sustainability practices help mitigate a wide range of risks, from supply chain disruptions to regulatory penalties.

Balancing Profitability and Sustainability

Balancing the financial bottom line with sustainability is easier said than done but it's more than possible with a forward-thinking mentality. In business, sustainability means building a model that's economically viable (profit) while protecting the environment (planet) and supporting fairness and well-being for everyone involved (people). These three pillars—profit, planet, and people—are deeply interconnected.

Ignoring one can easily throw the others off balance. Cutting corners on environmental or labor standards might save money now but can hurt a company's reputation and stability later. Or, going all in on sustainability practices might come at an insurmountable cost and drive profits too far down to stay in business.

The key is finding ways to align these priorities. It may require playing the long game but, when done right, balancing these pillars not only creates a sustainable business—it creates one that's built to thrive.

Environment, Social Governance (ESG) - A Global Issue

Companies are expanding the metrics they use to define success well beyond profit and sales. In response to growing concerns among their employees, customers, investors, and impacted communities, many firms are making themselves accountable for their Environmental, Social, and Governance (ESG) practices. Mainstream investors once considered such measures "non-financial," but have come to understand both related risks and opportunities - and are demanding more related data. The amount of ESG information being made available by rating agencies, technology firms, and auditing and consulting firms has exploded as a result, and efforts are afoot to bring more coherence and consistency to it through standards and regulation.

Improve your ESG performance and generate quantified triple bottom line results: People, Planet, Profit. A good sustainability strategy goes beyond ESG reporting. Identify the relevant ESG metrics, build a solid monitoring system and establish a governance from which corporate leaders can make sound strategic decisions. With the right strategy in place, you will improve your ESG performance and reap the positive results generated on People, Planet, Profit. Below are few guidelines to help you answer:

- What ESG metrics are relevant to my business and industry?

- How do we measure and keep track of ESG metrics while ensuring engagement and ownership at all levels of our organization?

- To improve on our ESG performance, which initiatives can help move the needle?

- What is industry best practices on ESG?

- How do we measure our greenhouse gases (GHGs) emissions?

- How can we measure and improve our Diversity, Equity, and Inclusion (DEI) efforts?

- Which reporting framework / standard should I use to ensure adequate disclosure based on current and future regulations?

"To deliver justice in the face of climate catastrophe; to help move us closer to securing a decent world for all humanity.

This is not a zero-sum game. And finance is not a hand-out. It's an investment against the devastation that unchecked climate chaos will inflict on us all. It's a down payment on a safer, more prosperous future for every nation on Earth. And so, we must make progress and we must use the progress we already made to build upon. I urge every party to step-up, pick-up the pace, and deliver. The need is urgent. The rewards are great. And time is short" - Antonio Guterres, Antonio UN Secretary-General".

Chapter 2

Education's Position at the Core of ESG: The Evidence-Based key to Social and Economic Outcomes

3 STEPS TO SEAMLESSLY INTEGRATING SUSTAINABILITY INTO CORE OPERATIONS

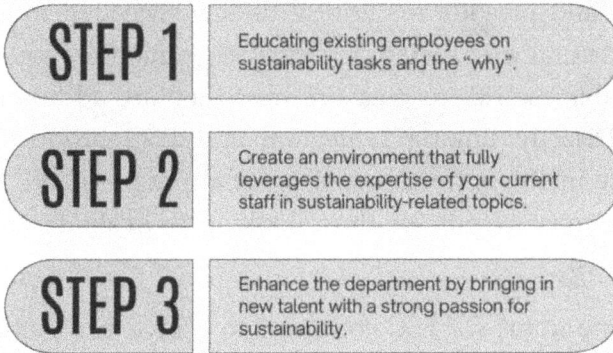

STEP 1 — Educating existing employees on sustainability tasks and the "why".

STEP 2 — Create an environment that fully leverages the expertise of your current staff in sustainability-related topics.

STEP 3 — Enhance the department by bringing in new talent with a strong passion for sustainability.

Sustain
&
Trend

Investment in Education has the power and ability to both improve society and drive business results.

Investment in Education, human development, and training is an investment in today and future generations. Positioning

Education at the core is a useful and impactful way to advance the objectives of companies and investors seeking to achieve better financial outcomes and improve Environmental, Social, and Governance **(ESG) performance and credibility.**

Currently, ESG is facing a crisis centered around the question of whether it is a risk framework or a method for improving performance with positive environmental, social, and economic outcomes. This debate has gained further attention with comments from industry leaders and CEOs, questioning the legitimacy and reliability of ESG.

"Greenwashing" claims and government inquiries into "green practices" of companies and investors have exposed ESG to increased pressure and scrutiny. To ensure that ESG continues to improve and provide the critical direction needed to advance environmental and social performance, companies need clear, quantifiable metrics to measure how they are addressing key issues. Directly linking Education and ESG produces more definitive methods for measuring social progress and, in turn, provides more depth for those looking to evaluate corporate ESG efforts.

As the importance of ESG continues to evolve, companies have the potential to identify and refine material ESG concerns, advance sustainability objectives, and mitigate short- and long-term corporate risk through investment in Educational initiatives that focus on lifelong learning. This will not only help to improve ESG performance but Investment in Education has the power and ability to both improve society, drive business results and provide the financial resources needed to address the Global Educational crisis.

In the last few years, the COVID-19 pandemic has deepened the Global learning crisis and contributed to a significant talent gap in the workforce. The pandemic increased the Global digital divide; decreased access to Education, particularly in underserved and minority communities; and laid bare the need for greater skills-based training. By 2030, there will be a "human talent shortage" of more than 85 million people.

Meanwhile, countries face stagnant growth, widening social and economic inequality threatening security and safety, supply chain disruptions, and intensifying Climate Change. Addressing any of these challenges is impossible if young people lack basic developmental milestones and skills needed to provide effective contributions in the workforce. These issues should be central to any company looking to establish a comprehensive approach to ESG.

A new approach to Educational investment that focuses on the link between Education and ESG - A new blueprint designed to yield benefits for companies and investors produced at the intersection of Education and ESG. Make a case for the materiality of Education to businesses and investors and call upon stakeholders to develop ESG programs guided by Education and integrating Educational programming into strategies with appropriate metrics to ensure investments have the intended impacts.

Commit to Urgent Action

Education, human development, and training — which encompass policies, programs, and activities ranging from early childhood development and literacy to formal Education for marginalized groups and skills for the workforce — present tangible corporate actions and well-researched, quantifiable impact metrics for evaluating performance. This allows for purposeful corporate action with measurable impact and results in not only social performance but across all three pillars of ESG.

Moreover, investment in Education, human development, and training is not only a necessity for today's workforce but an essential investment for future generations. All available data make it clear that positioning Education equity at the core of corporate social policies is a valuable and impactful way to advance the objectives of companies and investors seeking to achieve better financial outcomes and improve not only social outcomes but all ESG metrics and credibility.

Create a Globally recognized public good to drive new investments in ESG that systemically promote equity in Education, improve societal outcomes and address material corporate issues like -

- **Build a Team of Advisors:** Gain insights by coordinating an advisory network of corporate executives across various industries, investment professionals, financial institutions, ESG rating agencies, thought leaders in Education, and Global reporting agencies.

- **Generate Solutions:** Build out evidence-based solutions linked to corporate material issues, including both internal policies and training, as well as external community-based programs.

- **Develop Metrics:** Create tangible, substantive metrics for each solution, demonstrating broader societal impacts and allowing companies to dive deeper into the "S" in ESG

- **Provide Evidence:** Maintain an ongoing and updated repository of the latest evidence, ensuring decision-making is driven by the latest data.

- **Track Good Work:** Develop a database of company performance based on Education metrics and provide rankings and ratings to highlight the top performers in EbA

- **Inform Investment Portfolios:** Work with financial institutions to create Education-focused ESG products for investors to incentivize increased investment in Education equity from the private sector.

Beyond Changing the Rules

The way through to a sustainable future requires policy change at all levels — local, state, National, UN, corporate, and in non-profit organizations and government agencies. To meet the needs of nine to ten billion people, we also need to change minds through Education and change the game through Sustainable Business.

Changing the game of business is core to any sustainability strategy. Why? No matter how many minds we change through Education, or how many rules we change through policy , at the end of the day it will be business that has to figure out how to get sustainability done. How do we get food on the table, keep the lights on, create Global universal access to health care, all for nine billion people, in ways that radically — radically-- reduce environmental impact? We need 90% cuts in all kinds of pollution soon — Global warming emissions, toxic chemical emissions, impacts on biodiversity, plastics pollution. At the same time, business needs to reinvent itself to treat workers, communities, and suppliers with justice and with respect. Is this possible? Can business really change the game?

Reimagining business in service to sustainability is a recent idea in political economy. Typically, business is seen as the problem, not the solution: companies pollute the environment, deplete resources and can sometimes exploit workers and communities. This pollution and exploitation are often viewed through the lens of "negative externalities" or "external social costs". The argument goes that businesses are forced, regrettably, to impose these costs on society under the pressure of market competition. Any business that tries unilaterally to address these issues will face higher costs and be driven out of business. The solution? Government needs to internalize those externalities through regulation and level the playing field, allowing all companies to do the right thing. The road to a sustainable future under this theory of change runs through an intelligent and effective regulatory state.

Globally, significant progress was and in places still is being made under this regulation paradigm. But in many regions of the world, including the US at the National level, political gridlock has limited regulatory solutions. Under these circumstances, sustainable business has emerged as a critical alternative pathway. The core idea is that through radical, often ecologically inspired design, companies can develop business models that both reduce pollution and promote social justice, making money while doing so. Sustainable business considers pollution and social exploitation to be technological and social design problems, rather than negative externalities. As such, these challenges can be solved through business model innovation. Rather than facing higher costs, the sustainable business view is that companies that creatively address environmental and social problems can actually lower costs, increase revenues, and outcompete dirty companies.

Education in Sustainability is to offer deep training in three key areas.

- Sustainability Vision- how can businesses find profitable opportunities where others see environmental or social costs?

- Leadership—given the vision, how to get a team behind it?

- Execution—. With a vison and a team, how to deliver?

An Educated Workforce Can Embrace Green Growth Opportunities -

Education's Position at the Core of ESG

Figure 1.15: The 7 categories of ESG strategies

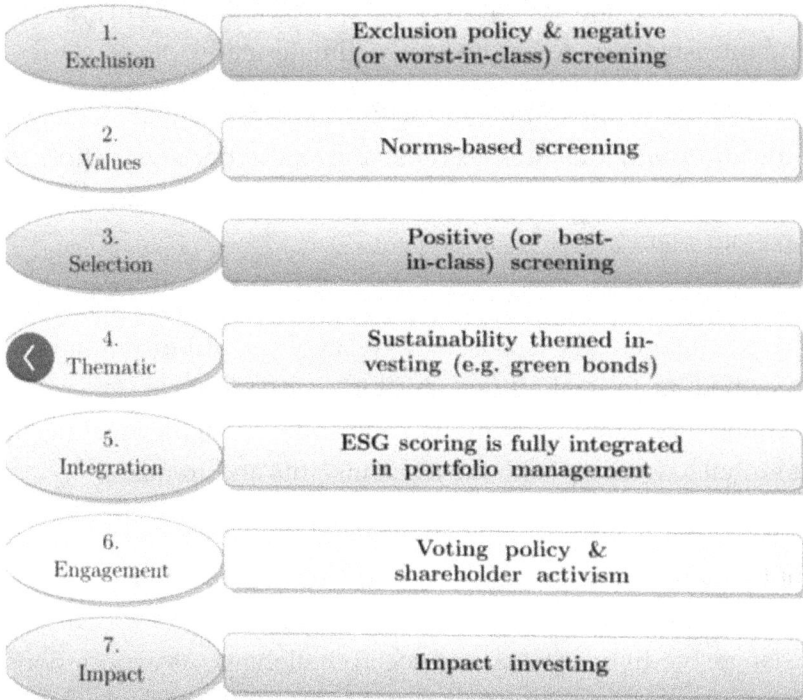

1. Exclusion	Exclusion policy & negative (or worst-in-class) screening
2. Values	Norms-based screening
3. Selection	Positive (or best-in-class) screening
4. Thematic	Sustainability themed investing (e.g. green bonds)
5. Integration	ESG scoring is fully integrated in portfolio management
6. Engagement	Voting policy & shareholder activism
7. Impact	Impact investing

An educated workforce is one possessing the skills, values, and desire to drive the technological transformation societies must deliver to combat Climate Change. Education can provide the basic, technical, managerial, and leadership skills necessary to innovate and develop green industries, transform economies and food systems, and reduce environmental destruction.

Green growth could produce up to 60 million additional jobs Globally, but for societies to benefit, they must have the workforce capable of filling these roles. This requires ambitious Education reform — from ensuring equitable access to quality early years Education right through to creating a commercial environment that nurtures and develops skilled professionals. Top level leaders shaping the policies underpinning Education systems can benefit from programs designed to deliver the capacity, skills and peer networks required to transform systems and infrastructure to become truly climate-ready.

We all have a role to play in the fight against Climate Change. Education and business leaders must take decisive action to shape the world's ability to adapt, innovate and ultimately to save our planet.

Knowledge sharing is one of the most powerful tools we have to drive change. As sustainability evolves rapidly, staying informed is crucial. From shifting regulations to emerging technologies, the landscape is constantly changing, making it essential to keep up with the latest insights and trends.

Sustainability is no longer just about compliance — it's about innovation, resilience, and impact. Companies, policymakers, and individuals are rethinking strategies to address Climate Change, biodiversity loss, and social challenges. As expectations rise, conversations around sustainable finance, circular economy models, and corporate ESG commitments are becoming more sophisticated.

The Big Question is from climate science and sustainable business strategies to ESG trends and the intersection of policy and technology valuable perspectives should be frequently read.

On innovation for inclusive growth -

Build pathways for trust-building and collaboration in areas including advancing technology, trade and investing, and antimicrobial resistance.

- By advancing insights and solutions in the above areas and also by -

- Exploring the effects of deGlobalization on firms, economies, innovation and societies

- Establishing guiding principles for technology policy

- Facilitating better data exchange within and across counties for cybersecurity

- Assessing the significance of metaverse technologies to industries and economies. We still need growth, but it's the quality of growth that matters,". "It needs to be green, and it needs to be inclusive."

- Defining growth not just in physical capital (measured GDP), but also in human capital (Education and skills), natural capital (climate and nature), and financial capital (access and assets).

- As Global shocks and advancing technology create new opportunities and risks, the case for investing in Education and skills to prepare people for future of work.

- "The skills gap is huge,"- "We have to change how we teach kids, we have to change Education, and we have to do training for our workers."

- Review long-term implications in inter-Sectoral and interdisciplinary manner -

- AI providers, educators, researchers, as well as parent and student representatives, need to collaborate on "system-wide adjustments" across curricula to both mitigate the risks and harness the potential of generative AI, says UNESCO.

- "We all need to be cognizant that GenAI might … change the established systems". AI tools should not undermine, conflict with or usurp us, states UNESCO. To ensure that doesn't happen, "the transformation of Education and research [by GenAI] should be rigorously reviewed and steered by a human-centered approach".

- The impact of Ai on the Education system and the need for changing assessment practices.

- How Ai is both a catalyst for change and a potential solution to the challenges posed by its presence.

- How Ai gives us the tools to assess self-awareness, self-regulation, metacognition, and other essential skills required for future-proof careers.

- How to gain insights from data to ensure that students are effective learners; that they are good at learning to learn.

- Advance insights and solutions in the above area by:

- Defining key concepts including equitable transition and

responsible investing

- Investigating potential future shocks and their impact on supply chains

- Creating fresh proposals for policy-makers to support efforts to drive good job creation

- Exploring investments, incentives and partnerships to advance social mobility and close gender gaps

On Collective Action for Climate and Nature

- Advancing insights and solutions in this area by:

- Unlocking and de-risking key investments and action across climate and nature systems

- Creating methods for evaluating air quality performance and trends

- Surfacing practical solutions to accelerate the pace of the energy transition

- Building an evidence-based framework for creating sustainable food and water systems

Can we Foster Global Peace Through ESG Practices?

In a world marked by geopolitical tensions, resource competition, and political conflicts, the quest for Global peace has never been more pressing. The Environmental, Social, and Governance (ESG) framework, which has gained prominence in recent years, offers a compelling path toward preventing wars by shifting our perspective from scarcity to abundance. By integrating ESG practices that prioritize abundance, we can take significant strides toward fostering a more harmonious and peaceful world.

Adopting an abundance mindset within ESG practices offers an array of strategies to avert conflicts and promote Global peace:

- Sustainable Resource Management

- Inclusive Social Practices

- Ethical Governance

- Innovation and Adaptability

- Responsible Investments

In today's fast-changing business landscape, companies face immense pressure from all directions — regulators, investors, customers, and even their own employees — to act more responsibly and integrate sustainability into their core operations. Environmental degradation, social inequality, and governance failures are no longer issues that can be swept under the rug. Stakeholders demand transparency, ethical practices, and long-term accountability.

This growing pressure has forced businesses to act more carefully, and it has brought us to the concept of ESG (Environmental, Social, Governance). ESG is CSR on steroids — while Corporate Social Responsibility (CSR) often reflects voluntary and broad initiatives, ESG represents a structured, measurable framework for businesses to assess and improve their sustainability efforts. It allows businesses to focus on specific, quantifiable outcomes that can be assessed and compared across industries.

While ESG is a business-centric framework, the SDGs offer a Global perspective, ensuring that businesses aren't just working in isolation but contributing to a broader collective effort. This is what we call the collaborative advantage – the power of unified action.

The development of partnerships with community groups, government bodies, and the private sector can catalyse research, empower communities and inform the policy making and action that the world needs to reach its climate targets.

A new approach to Educational investment that focuses on the link between Education and ESG. A new blueprint to yield benefits for companies and investors. Investment in Education has the power and ability to both improve society and drive business results.

Investment in Education, human development, and training is an investment in today and future generations. Positioning Education at the core is a useful and impactful way to advance the objectives of companies and investors seeking to achieve better financial outcomes and improve Environmental, Social, and Governance (ESG) performance and credibility.

Currently, ESG is facing a crisis centered around the question of whether it is a risk framework or a method for improving performance with positive environmental, social, and economic outcomes. This debate has gained further attention with comments from industry leaders and CEOs, questioning the legitimacy and reliability of ESG. "Greenwashing" claims and government inquiries into "green practices" of companies and investors have exposed ESG to increased pressure and scrutiny. To ensure that ESG continues to improve and provide the critical direction needed to advance environmental and social performance, companies need clear, quantifiable metrics to measure how they are addressing key issues. Placing ESG in Education investments can produce more definitive methods for measuring social progress and, in turn, provides more depth for those looking to evaluate corporate ESG efforts.

As the importance of ESG continues to evolve, companies have the potential to identify and refine material ESG concerns, advance sustainability objectives, and mitigate short- and long-term corporate risk through investment in Educational initiatives that focus on lifelong learning. This will not only help to improve ESG performance but also Investment in Education has the power and ability to both improve society and drive business results. It also provides the financial resources needed to address the Global Educational crisis.

In the last few years, the COVID-19 pandemic has deepened the Global learning crisis and contributed to a significant talent gap in the workforce. The pandemic increased the Global digital divide; decreased access to Education, particularly in underserved and minority communities; and laid bare the need for greater skills-based training.

By 2030, there will be a "human talent shortage" of more than 85 million people. Meanwhile, countries face stagnant growth, widening social and economic inequality threatening security and safety, supply chain disruptions, and intensifying Climate Change. Addressing any of these challenges is impossible if young people lack basic developmental milestones and skills needed to provide effective contributions in the workforce. These issues should be central to any company looking to establish a comprehensive approach to ESG.

We offer a new approach to Educational investment that focuses on the link between Education and ESG. We propose the development of a new blueprint designed to yield benefits for companies and investors produced at the intersection of Education and ESG. We also make a case for the materiality of Education to businesses and investors and call upon stakeholders to join us in developing ESG programs guided by Education and integrating Educational programming into strategies with appropriate metrics to ensure investments have the intended impacts.

Environmental challenges, including Climate Change, are changing the way businesses work, either because they are forced to or because they proactively seek to. Green businesses are more profitable and future proof. They save scarce resources, help maintain healthy ecosystems, minimize pollution and waste, limit greenhouse emissions, and provide green goods and services that enable more responsible consumption patterns. Green businesses are vital for a development model that delivers a triple bottom-line of prosperity, planet and people. However, sustainability as a business driver is novel, and companies will need support in the process.

Capacitate business service providers to support companies in the process towards greening the economy. The benefits from flourishing green businesses are twofold. The business community becomes more competitive while at the same time the jobs produced are supporting a societal change towards greener and healthier lives for people. Therefore, governments and private sector support agencies have a clear role and motive to promote greening of businesses and create an enabling environment for green business and job growth. Developed and middle-income countries are leading the way in supporting green business development, while a number of low-income countries are also taking positive steps. How do they do this? What works and what does not work in supporting green business development? Let us go ahead.

What does sustainable future mean to you?

A sustainable future for our planet entails a harmonious balance between human well-being, economic prosperity, and environmental health. Here's a vision of what it could look like:

1. **Renewable Energy:** Our energy needs are primarily met through renewable sources such as solar, wind, hydro, and geothermal power. Fossil fuels are phased out, reducing greenhouse gas emissions and mitigating Climate Change.

2. **Circular Economy:** We embrace a circular economy model where resources are used efficiently, waste is minimized, and materials are recycled or repurposed. This reduces strain on natural resources and minimizes pollution.

3. **Biodiversity:** Efforts to protect and restore ecosystems are widespread, ensuring biodiversity thrives. This includes preserving habitats, combating deforestation, and preventing the extinction of species.

4. **Sustainable Agriculture:** Agriculture practices prioritize sustainability, with a focus on regenerative techniques that enhance soil health, conserve water, and minimize chemical inputs. Local and organic food systems thrive, reducing food miles and carbon emissions.

5. **Green Transportation:** Transportation systems prioritize public transit, walking, and cycling, supplemented by electric vehicles powered by renewable energy. Urban

planning emphasizes compact, walkable communities to reduce the need for car travel.

6. **Water Security:** Water resources are managed sustainably, ensuring equitable access for all while safeguarding water quality and ecosystem health. Efficient irrigation practices and water-saving technologies are widely adopted in agriculture and industry.

7. **Climate Resilience:** Communities are equipped to adapt to the impacts of Climate Change, such as sea-level rise, extreme weather events, and shifting growing seasons.

   Climate-resilient infrastructure and disaster preparedness measures are in place.

8. **Green Technology Innovation:** Investment in green technology and innovation drives continuous improvement in sustainability practices across all sectors, from energy and transportation to manufacturing and construction.

9. **Social Equity and Justice:** Sustainability efforts prioritize social equity and justice, ensuring that benefits are shared equitably and vulnerable communities are not disproportionately affected by environmental degradation or Climate Change.

10. **Global Collaboration:** Countries collaborate on a Global scale to address shared environmental challenges, such as Climate Change, biodiversity loss, and pollution. International agreements and partnerships promote cooperation and collective action.

Achieving this vision of a sustainable future requires concerted effort and collaboration across all sectors of society, from governments and businesses to civil society organizations and individuals. However, the benefits - including improved public health, economic prosperity, and a thriving natural environment - make it a goal worth pursuing.

In a sustainable future, various aspects of societal life will undergo significant transformations, encompassing everything from how we consume energy and resources to how we interact with the environment and each other.

1. A Shift in the Energy Matrix:

The energy matrix will be predominantly composed of renewable sources like solar, wind, geothermal, and hydroelectric power.

- Innovative energy generation and storage technologies, such as more efficient solar panels and long-lasting batteries, will be widely utilized.

- Energy efficiency will be prioritized across all sectors of society, with the implementation of measures to reduce consumption.

2. Embracing the Circular Economy:

- The circular economy will become a dominant model, focusing on the reuse, recycling, and recovery of materials.

- Conscious and responsible consumption will be encouraged, leading to reduced waste and increased value placed on durable and repairable products.

- New business models based on the circular economy will

be created, generating employment opportunities and economic growth.

3. **Environmental Preservation:**

- Biodiversity will be protected and restored, with measures implemented to conserve natural habitats and endangered species.

- Sustainable agriculture practices will be widely adopted, minimizing environmental impact and ensuring food security.

- Climate Change will be combatted through measures to reduce greenhouse gas emissions and adapt to their effects.

4. **Social Inclusion and Equity:**

- Social inequality will be reduced, with universal access to basic services like Education, healthcare, and housing.

- Inclusion of all social groups will be promoted, tackling discrimination and guaranteeing equal opportunities for everyone.

- Global governance will be strengthened, focusing on International cooperation to address Global challenges like poverty, hunger, and Climate Change.

5. **Technological Advancements:**

- Technology will play a fundamental role in building a sustainable future, with innovative solutions developed to address societal challenges.

- Artificial intelligence, biotechnology, and nanotechnology will be utilized to promote sustainability in various sectors, including health, energy, and agriculture.

- Access to technology will be democratized, ensuring that everyone can benefit from its advancements.

The SDG curricular premise is that increasingly and at scale, businesses will profit by providing goods and services that yield: "shared well-being on a heathy planet". The Sustainable Business paradigm is not a Utopian vision. On the contrary it has inspired thousands of company to develop practical tools that are reorienting capitalism towards real problem solving, and away from a focus on short term profitability.

Chapter 3

The 5 Key Pillars of Responsible Business

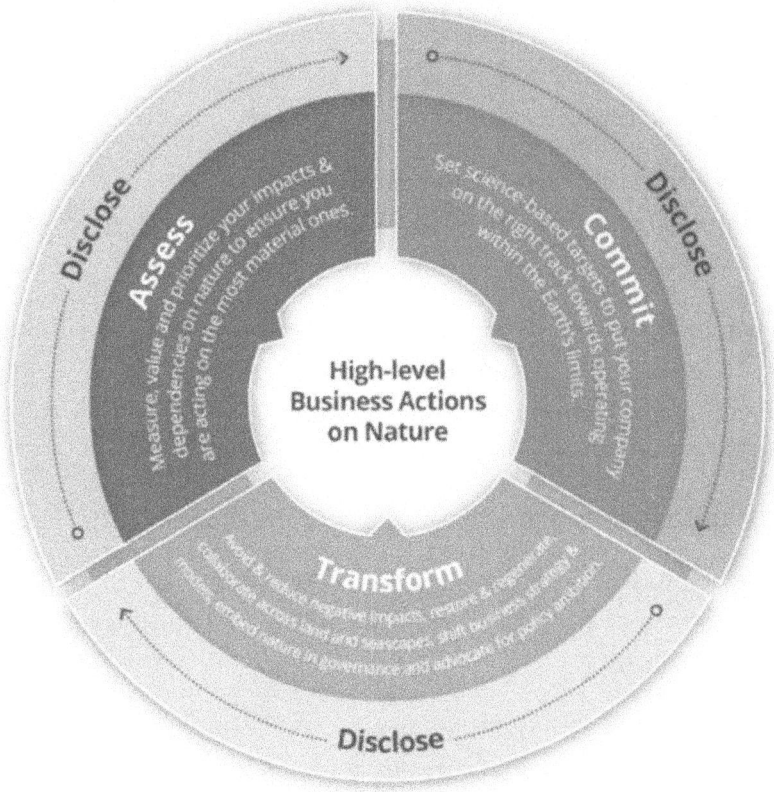

High-level Business Actions on Nature

Disclose

Assess — Measure, value and prioritize your impacts & dependencies on nature to ensure you are acting on the most material ones.

Commit — Set science-based targets to put your company on the right track towards operating within the Earth's limits.

Transform — Avoid & reduce negative impacts, restore & regenerate, collaborate across land and seascapes, shift business models & impacts, embed nature in governance and advocate for policy ambition.

Disclose

Disclose

Integrating Sustainability: Understand how to get companywide buy-in for the integration of sustainability and incentivize employees to act on initiatives.

Data Collection, Analysis and Management: Discover how companies are collecting high quality data to achieve a sharper insight into their impacts, including scope 3 emissions, to meet the incoming regulatory requirements and ensure decisions are made from accurate and transparent sustainability data.

Navigating Reporting Regulation: Hear from corporate peers, standard setters and industry experts on how to navigate change and prepare your business and value chain to be fit for a sustainable future.

Delivering a Net Zero Business: Discover the latest technologies, investments and nature-based solutions you can utilise to facilitate and accelerate the net zero transition.

Authentic, Impact-Driven, Communications: Discover how to communicate effectively with clear, digestible, and engaging sustainability communications that meet the increased demands and scrutiny from investors, employees and customers.

Integrating sustainability throughout the business

- How CEOs are leading from the front and empowering business leaders to embed sustainability throughout the business·

- Discover innovative ways of creating decentralised sustainability advocates that help deliver a consistent and fully integrated sustainability strategy

- How C-Suite leaders can frame sustainability as a departmental imperative, from legal and procurement to finance and innovation

- Build a resilient roadmap to accelerate the transition

- Learn how C-Suite executives are incorporating robust and agile net zero transition strategies into the wider business growth plans · Discover how companies are utilizing new tools and technologies to help plan and scale the investment in new climate technologies and innovations·

- Explore how businesses are identifying cross-industry collaborations that can accelerate impact and scalability, whilst reducing risks and upfront investments

- Zero carbon value chains

- How companies can adapt to their supply chain practices in recognition that scope 3 data and impacts are no longer a nice-to-have, but it's critical for business.

- Understand how Chief Supply Chain Officers and Chief Procurement Officers are helping deliver greater impact and high-quality sustainability data without impacting other key supply chain KPIs

- Critically examine new technologies that are helping companies collect and manage high volumes of data that is fit for the ever-increasing demands of sustainability reporting

Sustainability Strategy

- Learn how innovative companies are implementing sustainability initiatives across their business to shape future strategy and investments decisions.

- How businesses can leverage corporate partnerships and collaborating with external partners to fully integrate sustainability throughout their organisation and supply chains

- Discover which new tools and technologies are supporting these initiatives

Charting a sustainable course through CSRD and ESRS

- Gain insights from General Counsels, Chief Sustainability Officers and finance leaders as they dissect what is material to a business facing the CSRD

- Come with clear objectives to help implement a plan how to create a business-wide approach to the collection of high-quality, verifiable sustainability data.

- Hear from policy makers on how to navigate the regulatory and standard changes and what to focus on in 2024 and beyond.

Track A – Navigating Reporting Regulation

Assurance driven agenda: CSRD, ESRS, EU Taxonomy and CFD

- Understand how businesses can allocate assurances, and whether they should sit under finance audits and sustainability audits

- Explore how this can be aligned to regulatory demands to streamline your reporting program

- Review the role technology plays in streamlining data to improve data quality assurance and highlight its value to meeting reporting deadlines

Double materiality: Evaluating the impact of business on the world

- Deep dive into how sustainability impacts society and the financial significance of meeting multiple standards to create value for all business functions

- Identify the financial risks and opportunities of fast-approaching regulations to enable your business to flexibly meet the latest sustainability requirements and minimise compromising profitability

- Gain new best practice examples of embracing double materiality approaches to unite finance and sustainability teams, ensure a smoother transition, and reduce the risk of turbulence within your business

ESRS Interoperability with GRI and ISSB.

- How policy makers are to navigate the regulatory and standard changes, understanding what to focus on in 2025 and beyond

- Come away with actionable insights on how to leverage existing Global reporting standards to meet the ESRS

- Gain insight into the future of regulatory reporting and ensure you are kept informed with the latest headline information, abating your team's workload

Exploring the legal landscape: Implications of the CSRD on business

- Alongside expert legal practitioners, examine the evolving frameworks and legal intricacies of CSRD and ESRS and their impacts on multi National organisations

- Assess the compliance challenges facing businesses with reporting, interpreting, and enforcing regulatory requirements and the associated litigation risks, from the perspective of the in-house legal team

- Highlight legal frameworks supporting responsible business practices and how legal teams must collaborate across functions to foster a culture of sustainability

AI's role in reporting: Finding true value from the hype

- Understand the current capabilities of AI when it comes to the collection, management and analysis of sustainability data and how its supporting improved decision making

- Discover real world examples of how companies are using AI to bring greater clarity and oversight of their emissions data

- What lies ahead? Dive into the future of Sustainability reporting generate ideas on the role of AI in sustainability reporting in the years to come

Ensuring sustainability is a business imperative at the Board level

- How to frame the commercial opportunities, and risks, posed by sustainability

- Use qualitative and quantitative data to ensure sustainability remains a short-term priority for the board, alongside other immediate disruptions

Track B – Delivering a Net Zero Business

Building a Resilient Net Zero Roadmap

- Learn how to build a net zero roadmap that is robust and ambitious but also sufficiently agile to evolve with technological innovations

- Discuss how to utilise your emissions data and other non-financial information to build a full understanding of your value chain, and prepare your future agility strategy

- Explore best practices from other industry executives on how to harness the relationship between sustainability and operations insights to identify potential areas of flexibility and innovation

Collaborating with Departments for Impactful Change.

- Understand the best ways to foster cross-departmental collaboration to enact long-term sustainable business practices

- Learn how to reduce the sustainability skills gap and resourcing issues by upskilling and educating existing employees to ensure they incorporate sustainability into their work

- Understand how to shape communications for different departments to foster a culture of agency and ownership of sustainability

Zero Carbon Value Chains

- Set your business to reach absolute reductions throughout your value chain

- How to help your suppliers tackle their emissions and your customers change their consumption habits

- How companies can shift narratives and nudging behaviors to educate consumers and upskill suppliers - bringing their value chain with them on their net zero journey.

Natural capital: Building Biodiversity into Long-Term Business Strategy

- Broaden your knowledge of technologies and initiatives available to those investing in their biodiversity agendas

- Share the importance of understanding your underlying climate risk exposure

- Take-away tangible examples of the benefits available to you if you build nature into the core of your net zero transition plan.

Track C– Integrating Sustainability

Sustainability integration: From Education to action and ownership

- Understand how to manage and incentivse other departments to move sustainability higher up their priority list, giving urgency to their role in delivering against sustainability goals

- How to implement sustainability KPIs at all levels of the business and understand the impact this has had on prioritisation and culture

- Receive real-world examples of how you can foster a positive culture-shift to drive change and impact at all levels of your business.

- The demand for social and environmental stewardship: why real impact matters for all stakeholders

- How to ensure stakeholders at every level are inspired by leaders to adopt sustainable, value-generating business practices ·

- Gain insights in how to expertly navigate challenging conversations and ensure sustainability front and centre with your entire value chain ·

- Learn how to collaborate with peers, drive collaboration and identify opportunities that generate real societal worth and business success; an imperative for the long-term sustainability of any Global business

Onboard and Informed: The Vital Role of the Legal Function in Sustainability

- Examine the key reasons why it's important for the legal team to be engaged – from an early stage, and part of the conversation – with key sustainability decisions and initiatives

- Explore how the role of your legal team is evolving, and how your General Counsel can be a key advocate for sustainability at the Board level

- Understand how legal teams can transform governance frameworks to achieve a more responsible, transparent and compliant business

Track D – Data Collection Analysis and Management

Data management: Driving performance beyond regulatory compliance

- Learn how to manage sustainability data across organisational departments – collecting and integrating ESG data from multiple systems

- Understand how better collection and management processes can ensure regulatory demands are met, and your reporting process streamlined

- Discover how to drive performance beyond regulatory compliance through operationalising insights from ESG data into targeted business actions

Identifying, Tracking and Managing the Collection of Scope 3 Data

- Learn from leaders in the space who are working across their value chain to collect consistent, comparable, high-quality scope 3 data

- Understand how you can leverage new technologies and ways of working with your supply chain to source high-quality scope 3 data that's accurate and stands to scrutiny

- Discover successful techniques to engage key suppliers who are at various stages of their data collection journey

How AI is Being Used to Address Key Environmental Impacts

- Understand how artificial intelligence applications can be applied to energy transformation, supply chain execution, and enhanced risk analysis

- How AI has the potential to supercharge the way in which companies tackle key environmental risks

Finance Keynote

Strengthen strategic alliances between finance and sustainability

- Discover how to strengthen the relationship between your Chief Sustainability Officer and Chief Financial Officer to prepare your organisation for long-term financial, purpose-driven success

- Learn to utilise the finance department's expertise on data collection and management to improve your non-financial reporting practices

- Conduct value measurements on sustainability and investments to help demonstrate its long-term value to the business

Investment Keynote

Mobilising capital to unlock green growth

- Gain insights from senior investors and industry leaders on how the current climate is impacting investment decisions across the market and your business can take advantage of increasing investment into green projects

- Identify new investments opportunities that will put your business on the path to net zero, today.

Biodiversity Keynote

Building regeneration into short, medium and long-term strategy

- Invest in regenerative business practices as part of

innovative, transformation-based business planning that's central to growth and long-term strategy

- View the risk and opportunity, posed by a regenerative strategy and how it's being increasingly critical to future success

Systemic Change Towards a Net Positive Future

- Explore the latest technologies and strategies that are paving the way for companies to go beyond neutral, and instead deliver net positive

- Understand how innovative companies are embracing a net positive approach that leads to the business thriving

- Get ahead of your competitors through an in-depth discussion on what a net-positive future entails and key next steps for future strategies

Carbon futures Carbon Removal Strategy

- Focused on the critical role of carbon removal in corporate sustainability strategies.

- For corporate sustainability leaders every company to be committed to reaching their net-zero goals.

Scaling Innovative Finance for Biodiversity

Species and habitat loss drives the loss of ecosystem services, upon which more than half of the world's GDP, $44 trillion, depends. While the opportunities to halt and reverse biodiversity loss are abundant, there is an up to $700 billion annual shortfall between the current levels of financial investment and the amount needed to adequately protect and restore natural ecosystems. The private sector has a unique opportunity to be part of leading a systemic shift toward nature positive outcomes by developing comprehensive nature strategies and financing activities that protect and restore ecosystems.

Bringing together corporates, investors, project developers, and market experts to: advance key debates, including:

- Examine how to move from intention to action, including how biodiversity credits can be one impactful tool for businesses to operationalize nature strategies

- Discuss what biodiversity metrics and measurement practices to adopt to ensure robustness, suitability, and high integrity

- Hear about recent developments and next priorities for leading biodiversity actors Capturing business value from your nature strategy

Managing a company's exposure to nature can reduce risk, create business value, and build organizational resilience. Specifically, explore how companies can act to capture business value from their nature strategy.

Understanding and managing a company's exposure to nature can reduce risk, create business value, and build organizational resilience. While the Taskforce on Nature-related Financial Disclosures have established a pathway for managing and disclosing nature risks, standardizing an approach to capture the business opportunity is in its nascent phase.

Bringing together business leaders from across sectors to determine tangible actions that companies can pursue to play both defense and offense on nature. Key topics to include:

- What strategies can companies take to create business value from nature?

- How can a nature strategy make an organization more resilient?

- What can we learn from companies that are making it work?

The sustainable future will be one of prosperity for all, featuring a healthy planet, a just and equitable society, and a vibrant and resilient economy. Building this future requires commitment and collaboration from all sectors of society, from governments and businesses to individuals and communities.

10 BASIC CARBON TERMS YOU NEED TO KNOW

1 CARBON CREDITS
Carbon credits are tradeable certificates that constitute an offset of 1 ton of CO2 or CO2e from the atmosphere.

2 CARBON EMISSIONS
The release of Carbon dioxide into the atmosphere. it can also be catchall term related to other GHG emissions when quantified and converted to CO2e.

3 CARBON OFFSET
A project or an activity that reduces or remove carbon emission from the atmosphere to compensate for unavoidable emissions produced by others.

4 CARBON TAX
An environmental tax or penalty regulated by the government that organizations have to pay for their excessive production of carbon dioxide and other GHG.

5 CARBON SINK
A natural or engineered resource that has the ability to store and remove carbon dioxide from the atmosphere.

6 CARBON NEUTRAL
Anthropogenic carbon dioxide emissions emitted into the atmosphere is balanced with carbon dioxide offsets from reduction and removal projects.

7 CARBON DIOXIDE EQUIVALENT (CO2e)
A metric used to calculate all GHG emissions. it combines all greenhouse gases in one. By comparing its global warming potential against CO2.

8 CARBON MARKET
There are two types: compliance market and voluntary market. Both of these markets conduct the trade of carbon credits.

9 CARBON REGISTRY
An organization that verifies and validates the reduction/ protection/ removal of carbon emissions, and issues carbon credits certificates based on its developed methodologies.

10 CARBON ACCOUNTING
The quantification of carbon emissions and reductions and reductions complements GHG accounting.

ESG Scoring: This Para introduces you to methods for evaluating Environmental, Social and Governance (ESG) factors.

✓ **Sustainable Financial Products:** This section helps explore

ESG-focused financial products, such as funds, green bonds, and alternative assets.

✓ **Impact of ESG Investing on Prices and Returns:** This chapter provides an understanding of how ESG influences financial markets and portfolio performance.

✓ **Impact Investing:** This section helps discover how to invest to generate measurable social and environmental impact, while achieving financial returns.

✓ **Engagement and Voting Policy:** This chapter helps you learn about the role of active shareholding in promoting sustainable corporate practices.

✓ **Extra-Financial Accounting:** This section helps explore the integration of ESG factors into traditional accounting frameworks.

✓ **Climate Risk and Modeling:** This chapter takes a deep dive into strategies and tools for assessing and managing the risks associated with Climate Change.

How to Use the UN Sustainable Development Goals Strategically in Businesses

How companies and investors are embracing the Sustainable Development Goals (SDGs) and using them as a strategic tool to assess risks and innovative opportunities.

Learn about the United Nations (UN) Sustainable Development Goals (SDGs) and how regulatory trends and government incentives affect them in different parts of the world

- Understand how companies and investors are embracing the SDGs and using them for innovation and investment

- Explore the use of the SDGs as a common language to communicate with stakeholders

- Examine how to use the SDGs framework as a strategic tool to understand your company's biggest pain points to determine risks and new opportunities

- Examine the link between the SDGs and ESG, as well as a company's purpose and licence to operate and grow

- Discover how Global events and megatrends have prioritized and accelerated the implementation of SDGs by businesses and governments

Solutions Marketplace

- **Assess:** How can companies identify and measure their impact on the natural world?

- **Commit:** What process can companies follow to set nature-based targets?

- **Transform:** Which immediate, mid and long-term steps can companies take to protect and regenerate ecosystems?

- **Advocate:** How can companies leverage their influence on policy, public opinion and markets to accelerate a systemic transition to a nature-positive future?

- **Finance:** Which financial mechanisms can companies, investors and asset managers leverage to incentivize nature-positive practices?

Learning Objectives

By the end of the session, the participants will be able to:

- Describe what constitutes the integration of SDGs into

business strategies.

- Indicate current corporate practices on how businesses are integrating the SDGs into their strategies, with a focus on C-suite/Board and supply chain management.

- Identify effective corporate reporting practices on how sustainability/SDG priorities are addressed in the business strategy

Learning the Impacts of Climate Change and a Board's Accountability

How Climate Change is impacting society, supply chains, and business models; strategies to fulfil growing expectations, investor-driven reporting initiatives and regulatory demands.

- Take a closer look at why and how Climate Change impacts the Global economic and socio-economic outlook.

- Learn how Climate Change affects businesses, supply chains, customers, employees and society

- Assess short-, medium- and long-term transitional, regulatory, insurance and political risks

- Discover how to seize opportunities within renewable energy, carbon markets and a just transition

- Discuss the concept of net zero and using science-based goals around emissions, such as Scope 1, 2, 3 and 4 commitments, actions and reporting

- Examine the growing expectations for asset managers, proxy advisors and investors around initiatives such as Climate Action 100+ and the UN Principles for Responsible Investment

- Learn how companies, investors, insurance companies and regulators are responding to growing demands for climate action

- Understand scenario analysis and disclosure expectations, as well as adaptation, mitigation, and transition strategies

- Learn about the relevant regulatory bodies and non-regulatory bodies: SEC (US), European Union, International Sustainability Standards Board and Task Force on Climate-related Financial Disclosures

How to Build ESG Oversight and Foresight

ESG integration in business requires a comprehensive approach. It goes beyond reducing emissions or improving governance, covering a wide range of interconnected topics across Environmental, Social, and Governance dimensions.

Environmental factors include biodiversity conservation, resource efficiency, circular economy integration, and climate risk adaptation, all of which influence long-term business resilience.

Social considerations extend beyond traditional corporate responsibility, encompassing workplace health and safety, fair wages, diversity, ethical sourcing, and consumer protection.

Governance plays a fundamental role in ensuring transparency, accountability, and ethical business practices. Key aspects include ESG-linked executive incentives, anti-corruption policies, and regulatory compliance.

Addressing ESG requires a systemic approach. Environmental risks often intersect with social and governance challenges, making an integrated strategy essential for meaningful impact.

This ESG Wheel provides a simplified representation of the many factor's businesses must consider. In practice, ESG management is highly dynamic and industry-specific.

Materiality varies across sectors, with different industries prioritizing ESG topics based on regulatory landscapes, stakeholder expectations, and risk exposure.

A structured ESG framework aligns sustainability with business objectives, ensuring compliance, resilience, and long-term value creation.

The challenge lies in operationalizing ESG strategies — moving from concept to execution with clear targets, measurable outcomes, and continuous improvement.

How to anticipate and respond to the growing demands for ESG disclosure and how to ensure effective identification and integration of emerging risks into ERM-frameworks.

- Learn about the growing expectations for disclosure around ESG topics and how companies are best responding to those demands

- Look at what investors are asking for and why does that matter

- Get under the skin of ESG in businesses to see the difference between greenwashing and successful corporate sustainability

- Uncover how ESG disclosure issues are leading to securities class actions and civil litigation

- Understand ESG ratings, rankings, indices and integration frameworks, as well as materiality risk and opportunity assessments

- Discover why financial materiality assessments are integral for companies to embed ESG in strategy and board oversight

- Anticipate future trends and new requirements, while learning how to integrate emerging risks into enterprise risk management (ERM) frameworks

- Scrutinize oversight, accountability and the role of the board committees

Understanding Human Rights and Environmental Issues in Supply Chains

How to evaluate human rights, environmental impact and supply chain goals, targets and strategies; includes identifying, assessing, and managing risks related to child labor, modern slavery, along with climate and social disasters.

- Learn about the impact of environmental and social disasters on supply chains, and how to identify, assess and manage important risks

- Examine whether child labur, forced labur, modern slavery or other human-rights issues exist in your business supply chain

- Understand the impact of your products on the natural world, such as water scarcity, air pollution and deforestation

- Come to grips with compliance, looking at existing and emerging regulations as well as how to disclose support for major International norms and soft law initiatives

- Understand how to create mutually beneficial long-term relationships with suppliers

- Learn how to avoid supply shortages and reputational setbacks, plus align procurement with incentives Creating Diversity, Equity, Inclusion and Wellness in the Boardroom and Beyond Expectations from investors and society to foster a pipeline of diverse talent; proactively address employee misconduct and workplace culture issues.

- Define the expectations from investors, proxy advisors, and society to encourage diversity in the workplace

- Learn how to foster a pipeline of diverse talent into and through your company and achieve diversity of thought

- Understand the full spectrum and business value of diversity, as well as the regulations around it

- Learn how to address employee misconduct and workplace culture issues

- Identify the many forms of diversity — including culture, race, religion, age, sexual orientation, gender, disability, socioeconomic background and lived experiences — and the value they bring

- Address the power of data, the barriers to progress and best practices for diversity, equity and inclusion (DEI) in the workplace

- Understand the importance of mental health and wellness at work

- Examine the relevant laws and regulations for DEI in a

business, looking at board composition and structure, oversight, accountability and the role of the board nomination committee

- Learn performance evaluation methods, incentives, and accountability

Gaining Trust: Anti-corruption, Integrity, and Transparency Best Practices

Changing risks and expectations associated with anti-corruption and ethical business practices; developing and testing the hallmarks of an effective anti-corruption compliance program, including steps companies can take to reduce fraud and corruption.

- Learn the changing risks and expectations associated with anti-corruption, integrity, ethical practices and transparency

- Understand the steps companies can take to reduce fraud and corruption at work, including facilitation payments

- Examine public and self-disclosure, including the importance of company reputation matter in decision-making

- Understand how to manage and oversee investigations

- Learn how to anticipate new forms of corruption, such as cybercrime and dark money, as well as the misuse of private and public goods

- See how to build public trust, relations and reputation

- Navigate the political involvement of companies and businesses

- Develop questions to ask management to test the robustness and effectiveness of its anti-corruption approach

Re imagine and Re Build Business Strategy in Alignment with Sustainable Development

First thing first, its imperative to get educated and develop a 360 degree understanding of digital sustainability. To accept the responsibility to bring the change within own as well client organization. Re define the purpose and mission of organization to include sustainable development, not only in its own operations but also as business model. Align Go to Market Strategy with sharp focus on sectors which impact 17 SDGs, such as Energy and Utilities, Manufacturing, Agriculture and Food Systems, Transportation and Logistics, Construction and Infrastructure, Healthcare and Life Sciences, Education and Training, Government and Public Administration, Waste Management and Recycling, Water and Sanitation, etc.

As a technology consulting, Managed Services, Cloud Services and Data Centre services business we can create huge impact at a scale in the way organizations imagine, scope, assess and consume technology for transformation. In fact, we already are actively promoting digital sustainability solutions for afforestation, precision, reforestation Agriculture, Smart Solutions such as Smart Metering, Smart Street lights, Smart parking etc, for Smart Cities.

Moreover, we already have innovated around cloud technology using AI/ML with focus on digital sustainability to automate the optimize usage of energy hungry IT infrastructure resources. This brings in more efficiencies in IT operations of any organization and reduces the carbon footprint. We are also in the process of curating digital sustainability solutions for focus sectors as mentioned above.

Digital Transformation will be purposeful and effective only when we use technology in the effective implementation of the SDGs in all the 196 member countries. This requires not only great synergy between all stakeholders across the planet but also across all 17 goals.

In all this the big alliances whether it is G7, G20, BRICS, IT alliances, Big Tech Companies, UN agencies, MDBs etc. must be in sync totally to carry forward the Dream Goals for the next decade and their after and work unitedly For Galvanising Green initiatives as One Earth, promoting inclusive growth as One Family and synergising technology for One Future.

Ethics vs Sustainable and Interconnected Digital Landscape

Cloud computing enables efficient resource utilization and scalability, reducing energy consumption. Edge computing optimizes data processing at the source, minimizing data transfer and latency. AI and machine learning enhance energy management, predictive maintenance, and resource optimization. Blockchain ensures transparent and secure transactions, crucial for sustainable supply chains and renewable energy trading. The Internet of Things (IoT) facilitates real-time data collection for smart city management, agriculture, and environmental monitoring. Renewable energy sources power data centres and devices, decreasing carbon footprints.

Moreover, digital twins simulate real-world systems, aiding in designing sustainable infrastructures and optimizing operations. These innovations synergize to create a foundation for a more sustainable and interconnected digital landscape. However, challenges remain, including ethical AI use, e-waste management, and ensuring equitable access to technology for all communities to truly realize the potential of sustainable digital transformation.

Industry 4.0 and SMART Technologies

Pathbreaking work in field of Big Data and Data Lake solutions, advance data acquisition practices leading towards precise predictive and prescriptive data analysis. Emergence of Smart Factories with extensive use of IOT, Analytics, AI/ML and deployment of energy efficient systems fueled by renewable energy. Core ERP systems adopted by industry that contribute towards its ESG practices. Complete ecosystem of Decision Support and Enabling System delivered thru innovative and sustainable cloud technology leads to accelerated sustainable digital transformation.

Understanding Responsible Use of Data, Cybersecurity and Digitalization

Ethical considerations of the use of data including big data and AI generated opportunities; includes exploration of data collection, stakeholder privacy concerns, and the ethical management of confidential information and disaster containment.

- Learn the business impact of the digital revolution, including the hybrid workplace, big data and AI-generated opportunities

- Examine the ethical use of data, including collection, stakeholder privacy concerns and managing confidential information as part of a company's cybersecurity strategy

- Consider the balance between increased organizational and personal data protection against using data for good

- Understand how cyber risks can affect whether stakeholders view a company as acting responsibly

- Learn about business continuity through disaster containment and recovery in the face of cyber-attacks

- Examine antitrust laws and stakeholder expectations, including how to manage online propaganda and "fake news"

- Understand how cybersecurity ties into the United Nations Sustainable Development Goals (SDGs)

Addressing Tax, Investment & Pay in an ESG-Focused World

How to question the socioeconomic impact of potential business decisions, and the impact on the business' reputation and longevity; what information is needed to make well-informed tax planning, executive pay, and capital investment and capital expenditure (CapEx) decisions.

- Learn the latest Global trends in taxation, investments and pay policies that will help drive ESG best practices at your business

- Uncover when tax optimization is no longer carried out in a responsible manner

- Understand the cost of ownership in a volatile world, looking at the dilemmas you face when making long-term investments

- Learn what information you need to make well-informed

capital investment and capital expenditure (CapEx) decisions

- Uncover how to incentivize leadership for ESG in the short, medium and long term

- Examine the ripple effects of the COVID-19 pandemic on tax, investment and pay strategies, including income inequality

- Look to the future changes in Global tax policies that will drive ESG investments

Maximizing Shareholder and Stakeholder Engagement Around Disclosure

Determining the material issues to manage and communicate to shareholders and stakeholders, including engagement strategies and trends in reporting.

- Learn and manage the material issues that you need to communicate to your shareholders and stakeholders

- Uncover how to deal with the rise of shareholder activism, including best practices in engagement strategies before and after the proxy season

- Examine common standards and frameworks, such as the International Sustainability Standards Board (ISSB) and Task Force for Climate-related Disclosures (TCFD) Study regulations and requirements, including the Sarbanes-Oxley Act, Dodd-Frank Act, human capital accounting and stock exchange requirements

- Look at future trends in reporting

- Becoming a Steward of the Future: Best Practices in

Corporate Governance

- What does the future of good governance look like? What is the role of the board in 1 - 5 - 10 years? What is the fiduciary duty?

- Learn what good governance means now, and how that will evolve in the future

- Get ready for the evolving role of the board, executives, shareholders and other stakeholders

- Learn what it means to be a steward of the future — including having good judgement, courage and asking meaningful questions

Understanding New Geopolitical Risks and Expectations for Companies

How megatrends, geopolitical and environmental concerns and human values are changing expectations of businesses - including COVID19; how new business models are creating a purpose-driven and regenerative approach to doing business in the 21st century.

- Discuss how major Global events, such as Climate Change, the war in Ukraine and ongoing pandemics, are changing stakeholders' expectations of companies

- Understand how business trends, such as the great resignation, the use of data and social justice are shaping the future of work

- Look at organizational purpose and how to ensure it adds value

- Study the tidal wave of guidelines, regulations and ESG

reporting frameworks that are impacting the ability of businesses to operate

- Examine new business models such as stakeholder capitalism, the circular economy, regenerative and net-positive businesses, and the 5th industrial revolution

- Understand how asset managers, hedge funds, high-wealth individuals and proxy advisors are impacting boards of directors and board agendas

- Study the fast-evolving views and understandings of fiduciary duty across regions

- Explore the role of board committees in embedding ESG in business strategy.

Dealing with Dilemmas: Turning Business Risks into Opportunities

How to plan for major disruptions to ensure resiliency and business continuity, balancing short-term and long-term goals, Objectives, and Accountability.

- Learn how to lead and plan to ensure business continuity during major disruptions such as geopolitical upheaval, Climate Change, pandemics, societal changes and digital innovation

- Identify how a board of directors can fulfil its critical strategic role and set the cultural tone from the top

- Understand how to balance short-, medium- and long-term goals, objectives, compliance and accountability

- Examine the board's role in shareholder and stakeholder communications, including creating trust and integrity

- Study how incentives can drive wanted or unwanted behavior

- Scrutinize oversight, accountability and the role of the board committees

- Learn how to address shareholder expectations, letters and proposals, ratings and rankings, activist investors, and disclosure expectations

What's the Role of a Chief Sustainability Officer (CSO) ?

A Chief Sustainability Officer plays a pivotal role in driving meaningful impact within organisations. Here are the 12 key responsibilities that define this role:

1. **Strategic vision and Leadership:** Align sustainability strategy with long term business goals.

2. **Sustainability Integration:** Embed sustainability into operations across all departments.

3. **Stakeholder engagement:** Collaborate with internal and external partners to drive initiatives.

4. **Policy and Regulatory Compliance:** Ensure adherence to ESG Regulations.

5. **Climate Risk Management:** Identify and manage risks and opportunities.

6. **Sustainability Reporting:** Provide transparent ESG performance metrics.

7. **Innovation:** Champion sustainable product and service development.

8. **Partnership Development:** Build relationships with

NGO's and government agencies.

9. **Supply Chain Responsibility:** Maintain sustainability standards across supply chains.

10. **Sustainable Finance:** Integrate sustainability into financial decisions.

11. **Employee engagement and Culture:** Foster a culture of sustainability through training and initiatives.

12. **Performance Monitoring and Metrics:** Track KPI's to ensure continuous improvement.

How is Your Organization Approaching Sustainability?

The "Grammar of sustainability": the alignment of Agrifood companies to SDGs

In the transition to sustainability, agrifood companies need to be facilitated in the adoption of self-assessment and monitoring tools to support them in the implementation of sustainable good practices.

We are living in a period characterized by the urgency to transform the complex systems that govern our societies. However, as the recent COP26 has shown, there is no unanimity of visions, strategies and tools to achieve goals such as climate neutrality and the 2030 Agenda. Having a political and regulatory framework to support the transition is a key element, as well as the contribution of the private sector and civil society.

Agri-food systems produce one third of gas emissions, having an important role in Climate Change and the health of the environment and humans. Producers and consumers need to be aware of their impact, in order to face problems and adopt solutions.

In this context, the synergy between companies and the world of research and innovation is fundamental. Indeed, agri-food systems require new technological, organizational, social and digital solutions to ensure safety, health, equity, resilience and sustainability.

Companies need to be supported in understanding how they place themselves with respect to the various sustainability issues, monitoring the targets achieved and the investments necessary to improve. In other words, agri-food companies must understand and implement the "grammar of sustainability" which consists in translating the various dimensions of sustainability into strategic objectives and concrete actions, and in knowing how to adequately report the results achieved.

At the same time, the advantages and opportunities of those who have already started the transformation process must be made even more visible, to make them realize that environmental and social sustainability also brings economic sustainability.

The Future is Fair: How Fairtrade is Building Fairness into our Sustainable Tomorrow Farmers are on the front line of Climate Change. For millions of farming families and communities worldwide, especially those in the Global south, the impacts of Climate Change are a daily reality.

Farmers are on the front line of Climate Change. For millions of farming families and communities worldwide, especially those in the Global south, the impacts of Climate Change are a daily reality. 80 percent of the world's food comes from 500 million small-scale farms. If they suffer, we all feel the consequences. Some studies suggest that a rise of just one degree could lead to reductions of between five and ten percent in the yields of major cereal crops.

Enter Fairtrade: Fairtrade's unique, two-pronged approach helps farmers become more resilient to Climate Change, whilst at the same time giving consumers, retailers and traders the opportunity to reduce their carbon footprint. All this is underpinned by the Fairtrade Climate Standard empowering farmers to confront Climate Change and build for a better, greener, and fairer tomorrow.

Chapter 4

Integrating The SDG's into Sustainability Reporting

Overview of Key Sustainability Reporting Frameworks and Standards

Carbon Disclosure Project (CDP)

Materiality Focus: Impact Materiality
Audience: Investors, customers, and purchasers

Overview: A global system for environmental disclosure, using a questionnaire-based approach to assess and score organizations (A–D) on key environmental themes: climate, forests, and water. Updated in 2024 to enable integrated and sector-specific reporting for high-impact industries.

CDP

Global Reporting Initiative (GRI)

Materiality Focus: Impact Materiality
Audience: Broad stakeholders, including communities, regulators, and investors

Overview: The longest-standing sustainability reporting standard, offering modular guidance through universal, sector-specific, and topic standards. It focuses on organizations' significant economic, environmental, and social impacts, ensuring comprehensive and stakeholder-focused disclosures.

GRI

International Financial Reporting Standards (IFRS) – ISSB

Materiality Focus: Financial Materiality
Audience: Investors and financial institutions

Overview: Developed by the International Sustainability Standards Board, IFRS provides globally comparable disclosures tailored to financial markets. Its first two standards, IFRS S1 (General Requirements for Sustainability Disclosures) and IFRS S2 (Climate-related Disclosures), incorporate TCFD recommendations and provide a baseline for climate and sustainability reporting.

ISSB

Sustainability Accounting Standards Board (SASB)

Materiality Focus: Financial Materiality
Audience: Investors and financial institutions

Overview: Sector-specific reporting standards for 77 industries, focusing on sustainability metrics that directly impact financial performance. SASB standards have been integrated into IFRS, and they complement financial reporting by aligning ESG disclosures with investor priorities.

SASB

Task Force on Climate-related Financial Disclosures (TCFD)

Materiality Focus: Financial Materiality
Audience: Investors, lenders, insurers, and financial regulators

Overview: A framework providing recommendations for consistent and decision-useful climate-related disclosures. It addresses governance, strategy, risk management, and metrics, helping organizations communicate the financial implications of climate risks and opportunities.

TCFD

Task Force on Nature-related Financial Disclosures (TNFD)

Materiality Focus: Financial Materiality
Audience: Investors, financial institutions, and businesses with nature-related dependencies

Overview: Expands the TCFD approach to include biodiversity, ecosystem services, and natural capital. TNFD focuses on governance, strategy, risk management, and metrics, addressing financial risks and opportunities linked to nature and biodiversity.

TNFD

European Sustainability Reporting Standards (ESRS) (under CSRD)

Materiality Focus: Double Materiality (Impact and Financial Materiality)
Audience: EU-regulated companies, investors, policymakers, and stakeholders

Overview: Developed under the EU's Corporate Sustainability Reporting Directive (CSRD), ESRS mandates comprehensive ESG disclosures aligned with EU policy. It requires companies to address environmental, social, and governance impacts and financial risks, fostering alignment with European sustainability goals.

ESRS

Explore the Global sustainability challenges that are addressed by the Global Goals and the business case for engaging with the SDGs. delve into the role of sustainability reporting in enabling sustainable development; and, trend, challenges and opportunities related to reporting on the SDGs.

Take a deep dive into practical aspects of integrating the SDGs into existing sustainability reporting processes by following the steps outlined in the publication Integrating the SDGs into Corporate Reporting: A Practical Guide, developed by the UN Global Compact and GRI. This course ends with guidance on how to use the tool An Analysis of the Goals and Targets, also developed by GRI and the UN Global Compact, that can be applied to find the appropriate indicators and GRI disclosures to report on the SDGs. By upholding recognized standards and principles on issues such as human rights, labour, the environment and anti-corruption, organizations make an essential contribution to the SDGs.

- Describe the Global sustainability challenges that we face as well as the business case for engaging with the SDGs

- Explain the role of sustainability reporting and how it contributes to sustainable development and the achievement of the SDGs

- Interpret the current trends, challenges, and opportunities faced by organizations when it comes to reporting on the SDGs

- Integrate the SDGs into your reporting process by following the steps outlined in the publication 'Integrating the SDGs into Corporate Reporting: A Practical Guide', developed by the UN Global Compact and GRI

- Describe the reporting experiences of organizations in different sectors after examining their case studies.

Be it consumers, regulators, or an increasingly selective workforce demanding that employers do more, businesses are feeling the tide turn towards sustainability as the basis for long-term business success, rather than a mere 'nice to have'. "This presents a huge responsibility and opportunity for leaders to challenge their existing operating structures and cultures – even their fundamental purpose and value proposition – and lengthen their stride into relatively unknown ways of doing business,"

Discovering the business case for sustainability and the value of strong leadership in driving sustainable practices through the below mentioned points -

- Know what the SDGs are, why they are important and how each individual can be an agent for positive change in the world;

- Understand the role of business in the transition to sustainable development to create a prosperous future for all;

- Be able to identify interconnectedness of the SDGs and the challenges behind solving them;

- Know how management insights can contribute to the SDGs;

- Be able to evaluate the effectiveness of current business strategies in contributing to the SDGs;

- Develop a positive, critical, aware and courageous attitude towards the SDGs.

- Investigate the impact of current Global economic, social, and environmental pressures on business in a local and Global context

- Argue the business case for sustainability and the value of strong leadership to drive sustainable business

- Justify the importance of integrating sustainability across an organisation's value chain to ensure long-term value creation

- Assess the potential of innovative design and technology to enable sustainable business

- Formulate a practical action plan for overcoming the barriers and seizing the opportunities associated with creating a sustainable business

The Future of ESG Reporting is Here—Standardized, Mandatory, and Full of Opportunity. Are You Prepared?

Sustainability reporting has changed a lot. What used to be optional is now becoming a must-have for businesses. Global standards are aligning, and companies are being asked to share clear, reliable ESG data. Here's what's happening:

1. ESG is no longer just about compliance.

2. It's about embedding sustainability into everyday decisions. Companies need to show they're serious about transparency and accountability.

3. Standardization is the new norm.

4. Governments and organizations are setting rules that make ESG reporting more like financial reporting. The goal? Clearer, comparable data across markets.

5. Challenges bring opportunities.

6. Yes, businesses need better systems and processes. But the

reward is worth it: stronger resilience, better access to capital, and more trust from stakeholders.

Takeaway: Companies that get ESG reporting right don't just meet regulations — they lead the way in building a sustainable future.

Are you ready to find out how you can be an agent for positive change?

Reporting on the SDGs with Double Materiality:

Enhancing Corporate Sustainability Despite significant efforts, Global progress on achieving the Sustainable Development Goals (SDGs) remains insufficient. While the SDG targets and indicators were originally designed for countries to measure their progress, the private sector also plays a critical role in driving these goals forward. Without active and strategic engagement from businesses, many SDG targets are unlikely to be met.

Despite the challenge of the SDGs being developed for Member States, they have resonated strongly with the corporate world. According to the Governance & Accountability Institute, Inc. 2023 research on sustainability reporting, 52% of Russell 1000 companies aligned with the SDGs in 2022 – an increase from 32% in 2019. From the 472 companies aligning with the SDGs, there were 4,170 specific mentions of one or more of the 17 SDGs, with S&P 500 companies making up the majority. This growing commitment is evident across key sectors such as Consumer Staples, Utilities, Real Estate, Materials, and Health Care. However, despite this strong uptake, there are significant challenges in how businesses integrate the SDGs into their reporting practices.

Companies can selectively report on positive contributions to the SDGs while overlooking negative impacts, leading to SDG-washing. Another standard practice in voluntary SDG reporting is that many companies tend to cherry-pick the SDGs that are easier to measure and report on, leading to incomplete and potentially misleading comprehensive assessments on the company's overall SDG performance. Furthermore, there is a significant lack of comprehensive reporting that assesses SDG impacts across the value chain. This selective approach undermines the credibility of SDG-related information and hinders stakeholders from making informed decisions.

A thorough understanding of the context in which they operate, impacts as well as financial risks and opportunities can help companies align their business strategies with Global sustainability priorities. By embedding the SDGs into double materiality assessments, businesses can ensure that their reporting is not only more accurate and credible but also strategically aligned with long-term business success. Moreover, adopting a double materiality approach can help companies advance strategic action on the SDGs, while also helping to uncover potential risks that could arise from ignoring negative impacts on the SDGs.

To ensure that current SDG reporting practices remain credible, relevant and actionable in a rapidly changing reporting landscape, businesses are urged to report on the SDGs through a double materiality approach. This comprehensive assessment allows businesses to set ambitious, SDG-aligned goals that drive meaningful progress and enhance their resilience and value.

To support companies in this strategic integration and equip corporate sustainability reporters with insights to seamlessly integrate the SDGs into their sustainability reporting practices, ensuring that their reporting and contributions to the SDGs are both impactful and aligned with the evolving Global reporting landscape.

- To explore current approaches and practices to integrating the SDGs into corporate sustainability reporting processes.

- To equip participants with practical insights that facilitate a deeper integration of the SDGs into sustainability strategy and reporting practices, with a focus on double materiality assessments.

- To engage participants in discussions with reporting experts on the implications of double materiality for SDG reporting.

- To foster a deeper understanding of the interplay between different reporting frameworks, with a focus on the GRI Standards, and how they can be used to drive disclosures on the SDGs.

Corporate sustainability reporters, with varying levels of reporting maturity (from beginners to experienced SDG reporting practitioners).

The Relevance of the SDGs for Business

- Why do the SDGs matter for business? (Introduction to impact and financial materiality)

- Overview of SDG progress, recommitment at the Summit of the Future, and implications for business

- Baseline responsibilities for business

- Enhanced understanding of the opportunities and

responsibilities the SDGs represent for business as well as the concept of double materiality.

Current State of SDG and Corporate Sustainability Reporting

- Trends in Global and regional sustainability disclosures regulation

- Gain insights into current trends in sustainability reporting and the implications and opportunities for SDG reporting.

The SDGs in Sustainability Reporting

- Overview of how SDGs are embedded in key sustainability reporting frameworks and standards

- The SDGs and the GRI Standards (incl. overview of tools that facilitate reporting on the SDGs (An Analysis of Goals and Targets)

- A clear understanding of how current sustainability reporting frameworks and standards, with a focus on the GRI Standards, align with the SDGs.

- Integrating SDG reporting is a straightforward process for organizations already engaged in sustainability reporting, thereby encouraging broader adoption and more effective disclosure on the SDG-related impacts, risks and opportunities.

Navigating the Interplay of SDGs & Double Materiality

- Bring together industry leaders and reporting practitioners to share their experiences and approaches to embedding SDG considerations into double materiality processes.

- Explore current approaches, challenges, and lessons learned in integrating SDGs into double materiality approaches and processes.

- Topics to be discussed:

- Starting with impact materiality

- Defining sustainability value creation

- Interplay between negative impacts and value destruction

- Integrating impact and financial materiality

- Evolving regulatory landscape

- Identifying material SDG-related topics

- Challenges in integration

- Measuring Impact and performance

- Gain a comprehensive understanding of how businesses are approaching the interplay of SDGs in double materiality assessments.

Climate and Nature Crisis: Time for Bold Action

6 Key Reasons Why Sustainability is Essential for Business

Risk Management
Effective sustainability practices help mitigate a wide range of risks, from supply chain disruptions to regulatory penalties.

Critical Times
We're facing unprecedented challenges like climate change, biodiversity loss, and social injustices. These issues are interlinked, requiring a comprehensive approach to sustainability.

Operational Optimization
Optimizing operations with sustainability in mind reduces waste, lowers costs, and enhances efficiency, making environmental responsibility a driver of long-term profitability.

Regulatory Landscape
The regulatory environment is rapidly evolving. Businesses that don't adapt could face fines, reputational damage, and missed opportunities.

Competitiveness
Companies leading in sustainability are setting the standard. To stay competitive, others must step up, as customers increasingly demand sustainable practices.

Investment Attraction
ESG performance is now a key indicator for investors. Platforms like eToro highlight how mainstream this has become—attracting investment now means excelling in sustainability.

Sustain & Trend

The climate and nature crisis stands as one of our most pressing challenges today. 76% of people agree it is the most critical issue facing our world, and 51% believe it will worsen in the next decade if we do not act now. The impacts of Climate Change are already being felt, from rising sea levels to extreme weather events, but it is future generations who will suffer the most. This is a call for bold action. We must stop financing fossil fuels and prioritise investments into a sustainable economic future.

Governments must be held accountable for their promises to protect our planet. Young people need the skills and opportunities to lead climate solutions. Realising these goals demands a Global shift in policy and practice, with collaborative action by all generations across the globe.

Education is a keystone investment into ensuring the realization of all Global goals, including Climate Change, diversity, equity, and inclusion, public health, and broad-based economic growth. Across the world, businesses invest hundreds of millions of dollars in Education in countries across the globe. Yet too many of these resources do not have an impact on learning and skill development.

A study from the Brookings Institution revealed that millions of dollars in business contributions to support Global Education from the Fortune 500 companies were small, short-term, uncoordinated efforts that were not reaching the most marginalized. Both how the business community channels its resources and how the Education sector works with the business community will play key roles in determining not only the future of Education but the entire Sustainable Development Goals agenda.

Integrated social impact strategies and ESG investing are critical ways that businesses can improve lives and meet societal challenges. Corporate responsibility is also increasingly important for companies to improve their bottom line and attract and retain investors, talent, and customers: 86% of employees prefer to work for companies that care about the same issues they do. Consumers are also demanding action on social issues from businesses: 83% of consumers think companies should be actively shaping ESG best practices. Now, more than ever, the world is looking to the business community to take social action.

Education works with the business community to incorporate sustainable and scalable investments in Education into their social impact, philanthropy, corporate responsibility, and ESG practices.

The private sector can (and should) lead the way on nature-positive.

Nature has seen collateral damage in the growth of the Global economy in the past few decades. Is it possible then for the private sector to lead the way to a nature-positive future? Not only is it possible, but it may be our best shot, and companies and investors need to step up.

Our Global economy, for all its sophistication, appears to have the enlightenment of soil bacteria. The genus Paenbacillus has been found to commit 'ecological suicide'. They do this by making their soil surroundings unsustainably acidic as their population density increases, resulting in complete collapse of the bacterial community. Sounds familiar?

Humanity's current economic model, at current course and speed, is leading us to ecological suicide. The recent geopolitical, economic and pandemic shocks notwithstanding; data on a host of wellbeing indicators shows that Globally, we collectively face fewer accidents, natural deaths, crimes, wars and less political oppression than ever before.

Just like the soil bacteria, amidst – or because of - human progress, we appear to be sowing the seeds of our own ultimate destruction. We are living through the sixth mass extinction of nature and the first caused by humans. Over a million species are at risk of being wiped out, taking with them essential life-giving services, putting our food and health systems at risk. Between 1992 and 2014, produced capital per person doubled, and human capital per person increased by about 13% Globally; but the stock of natural capital per person declined by nearly 40%.

The world lost an estimated USD 4 to 20 trillion per year in ecosystem services from 1997 to 2011. No CEO would ignore a systemic risk of this magnitude.

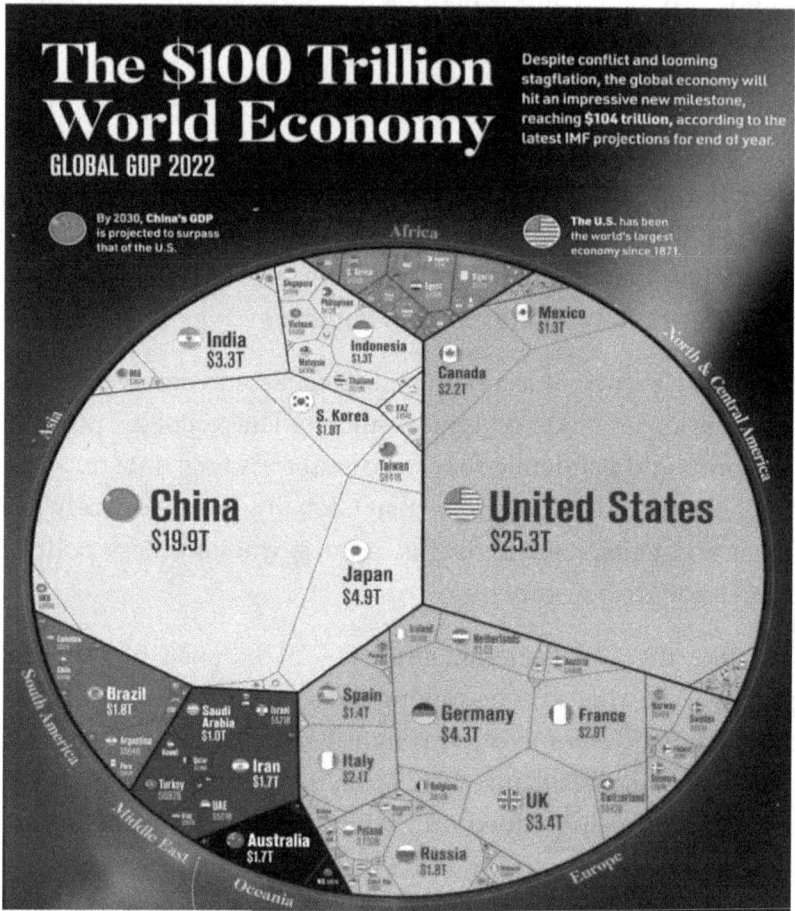

The $100 Trillion World Economy
GLOBAL GDP 2022

Despite conflict and looming stagflation, the global economy will hit an impressive new milestone, reaching **$104 trillion**, according to the latest IMF projections for end of year.

By 2030, **China's GDP** is projected to surpass that of the U.S.

The U.S. has been the world's largest economy since 1871.

Africa

India $3.3T

Indonesia $1.3T

Mexico $1.3T

Canada $2.2T

S. Korea $1.8T

Taiwan

China $19.9T

United States $25.3T

Japan $4.9T

Brazil $1.8T

Saudi Arabia $1.0T

Iran $1.7T

Spain $1.4T

Germany $4.3T

France $2.9T

Italy $2.1T

UK $3.4T

Australia $1.7T

Russia $1.8T

Asia / North & Central America / South America / Middle East / Oceania / Europe

The economic model that has made this progress possible but also put the planet at peril is broadly capitalist in nature, with private enterprise featuring prominently. Is it possible then for the private sector to help get us out of this mess? Not only is it possible, but it may be our best shot, and companies and investors need to step up and lead the way.

For starters, we can now put numbers to the economic loss from the nature crisis, which helps capture quantitatively inclined business minds.

Similarly, we also now have numbers for the upside: the money that stands to be made in a nature-centric approach to business. It is estimated that transitioning towards nature-positive economic models in key sectors could generate almost 400 million jobs and more than USD 10 trillion in annual.

Business value by 2030. Again, this is hardly an investment proposition on its own, but it's certainly a compelling frame for interesting investment ideas.

How then should companies and investors act so they manage the risks, seize opportunities, and lead the way to a nature-positive future? As a mining industry, we are far from having cracked this nut (pun unintended), but we have learnt a few things worth sharing. Unfortunately, few other industries have made the commitment to keep the most critical areas off-limits and strengthen the duty of care for protected areas. First, it is important to define and commit to 'no-go' areas; that is, to safeguard areas of outstanding universal and high biodiversity value from development. Members of the ICMM – 26 companies representing one-third of the Global mining industry – have since 2003 voluntarily committed not to mine or prospect in World Heritage sites. This was more than 10 years before the United Nations' Sustainable Development Goals (SDGs 11 and 15) called for a strengthening of efforts to protect and safeguard the world's natural heritage.

There's clearly room for leading companies and investors to step up, individually and collectively, to keep the most critical areas off-limits and strengthen the duty of care for protected areas.

The biggest impact however would come from governments legislating against industrial activity in these areas of outstanding universal value – and that change could not come soon enough.

Second, reframing the context can unlock new opportunities. ICMM members are committed to applying the mitigation hierarchy at operations to minimise impacts with the ambition of achieving no net loss of biodiversity. However, we know that no net loss is not enough given the scale of the nature crisis, and this is where changing the frame can help. In our case, extending our focus from the mine site towards landscape-scale approaches and from biodiversity towards integrated nature, social and climate goals is starting to unlock new pathways to contribute to nature-positive societies around the world.

We realise that we cannot do this alone and that working with others at the landscape level will be critical in halting and reversing the loss of nature. That won't be easy – multi-stakeholder initiatives rarely are – but it's the best chance we have of lasting change, at scale.

National accounting systems fail to reflect the economic value of nature. Private sector and voluntary leadership is perhaps our best hope of correcting this failure.

CARBON FOOTPRINT

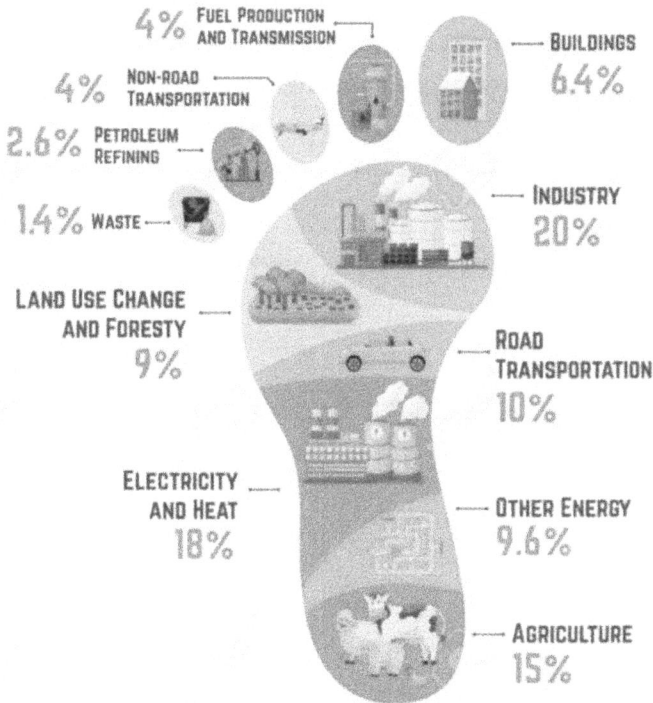

4% FUEL PRODUCTION AND TRANSMISSION

4% NON-ROAD TRANSPORTATION

2.6% PETROLEUM REFINING

1.4% WASTE

LAND USE CHANGE AND FORESTY
9%

ELECTRICITY AND HEAT
18%

BUILDINGS
6.4%

INDUSTRY
20%

ROAD TRANSPORTATION
10%

OTHER ENERGY
9.6%

AGRICULTURE
15%

Finally, investing in the quality of information to guide decisions is critical. The Dasgupta Review, amongst others, links the nature crisis to the fact that our National accounting systems like Gross Domestic Product (GDP) fail to reflect the economic value of nature. Here too, private sector and voluntary leadership is key and perhaps our best hope of correcting this failure.

Defining and valuing our impacts and dependencies on nature is the first step in course-correcting Global financial flows towards a more nature-positive future. Initiatives like the Taskforce on Nature-related Financial Disclosures (TNFD), which ICMM is proud to support as a piloting partner, are critical efforts in this regard which deserve maximum support.

These three areas hopefully provide a basis for a bold private sector leadership and collaboration at this critical juncture and can provide progressive governments with additional support to aim for the most ambitious outcomes in near future.

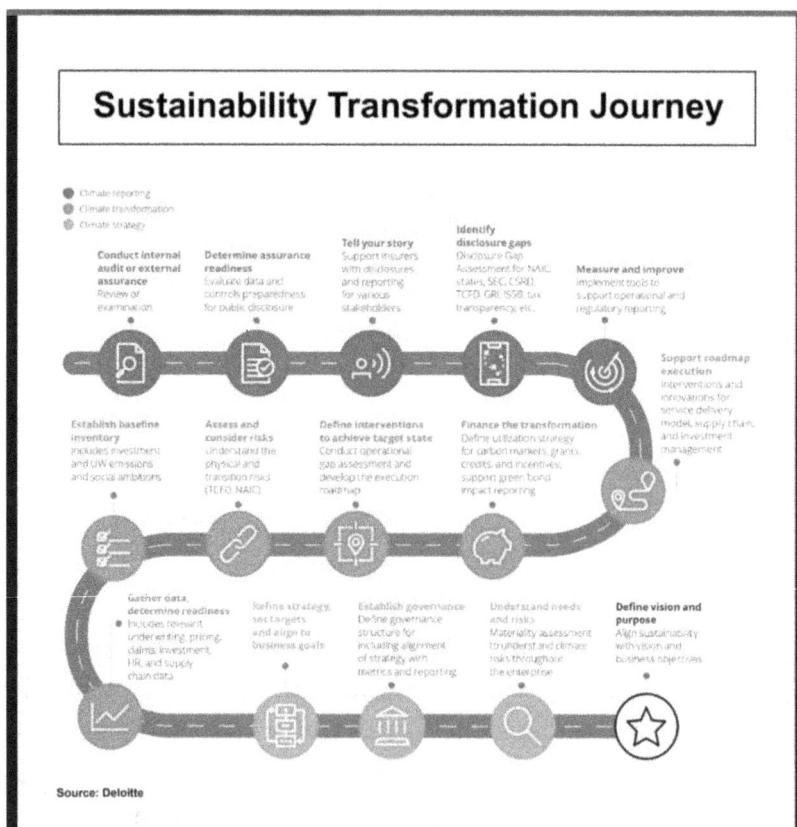

Sustainability Transformation Journey

Source: Deloitte

Business Groups Engagement for Quality Technical and Vocational Education Training (TVET)

The private sector has an important role to play in promoting quality TVET both as an employer and a training provider. Aligning existing TVET programmes to industry demand is a top priority as the world of work and training prepares for the post-COVID-19 'new normal'. Despite being such key players in TVET reform and implementation at the country level, companies and other development partners have limited venues for interaction and knowledge exchange at a Global level. They are often working towards a similar goal – improving the quality of TVET –but have not been visible partners to each other.

UNESCO-UNEVOC recognizes the importance of fostering discussion and engagement with companies (Global, local, small and medium-sized enterprises) to ensure TVET is demand-driven and future-focused. To facilitate this collaboration, UNESCO-UNEVOC is working to create a Global platform for partnership between private companies and the development community. This platform will provide opportunities for both parties to prepare for the future of work and TVET collectively, and to synergize respective investments at the country level.

To maximize impact, UNESCO-UNEVOC will prioritize the industries most likely to be disrupted by the processes of digitalization, automation and greening.

The TVET programme will bring students from a variety of fields together, to study and work in multidisciplinary teams and create novel sustainable solutions for human, urban, industrial and business environments.

The pedagogical approach is based on integrating teaching and research, problem-based learning, design thinking, blended learning and strong connections to practical outcomes.

The importance for young people to acquire digital and Sustainable skills:

"Digital skills are the work-place tools now and in the future. Everyone must develop these skills in order to be able to either access training remotely, navigate in their everyday life where services for citizens are digitized, and have more opportunities for employment, since digital technology is present in almost all economic sectors and occupations."

1. Five Ways to Unlock SDG Progress

We are at the midway point on the journey that started in 2015 with the creation of the United Nations' Sustainable Development Goals. The goals, 17 in all, aim to address some of society's toughest challenges, including eradicating poverty, increasing lifespans and health, and tackling Climate Change.

But progress has been slower than we would have liked. Although we have seen lasting gains in areas related to some basic needs — for example, electricity and internet access — the COVID-19 pandemic marked a major setback. Related developments such as spikes in inflation and interest rates, as well as Global events including Russia's invasion of Ukraine, have created additional stress around issues such as food security and economic development.

Of the roughly 140 SDG-related targets for which data is available, only 12% are on track to be delivered by 2030. Some 50% are advancing slowly. And for more than 30% we see either stalling or even reversal of progress. All told, not one SDG has yet been achieved.

It's not too late, however, to deliver on the SDGs. The world has more resources and capabilities to advance the human condition than at any time in history. We see five areas where action at scale can unlock rapid SDG progress:

- Digital. Data and decision-making technologies are not new. But the tools at our disposal are radically better than they were even five years ago. Global data commons and public digital infrastructure have become as critical to human success as physical infrastructure. Advanced decision support tools (powered, for example, by satellite data) can drive effective localized solutions. Technology can be an even more incredibly powerful driver of progress.

- Private-Sector Engagement. When companies identify business models that both address social issues and create competitive advantage, those solutions can scale quickly. One need only look at the takeoff of the electric vehicle market and the impact that is having on emissions to understand the magnitude of potential private-sector impact. We see this potential for scalable private-sector impact across almost all SDGs.

- In-Country Collaboration. Programs and initiatives for most SDG goals will only work if they are delivered with deep local insight and the engagement of the beneficiaries. Building capabilities at the country level can marry local execution with Global expertise and funding to achieve impact at scale.

- Innovative Financing. Achieving the SDGs will require

large amounts of capital. That makes the role of blended finance — which must become even more commonly utilized and innovative — a powerful lever for maximizing impact.

- Climate Adaptation and Resilience. The SDGs aim to address issues facing people and the planet. Adaptation and resilience (A&R) sits at that nexus. Worsening Climate Change has ripple effects that put many of the SDGs further out of reach. Investments in A&R — based on data and accompanied by strong implementation — can stem and even reverse that dynamic.

- The efforts and enablers listed here have proven effective at advancing many of the SDGs — and they could make a major difference if scaled. We should focus today on fully leveraging these opportunities. Together we can reignite momentum toward the SDGs and help create a more sustainable and equitable world for all.

2. We Can't Meet the SDGs Without Climate Adaptation and Resilience

Extreme heat, floods, droughts, rising sea levels, and other shifting climate patterns pose significant threats to the most vulnerable communities and populations — particularly in the developing world. These impacts, if not adequately addressed, put the Sustainable Development Goals further out of reach.

The World Bank warns that Climate Change could force 130 million more people into poverty within a decade. That creates major headwinds for achieving SDGs related to eliminating poverty (SDG #1) and promoting decent work and economic growth (SDG #8). Sensitive natural ecosystems, such as forests and wetlands, are also at risk of being upended by climate hazards—with direct implications for progress on protecting our environment (SDG #14 and SDG #15). A changing climate also makes it more difficult to end hunger (SDG #2), advance good health (SCG #3), and ensure access to clean water (SDG #6).

These dynamics make it clear that, if we are to reach the ambitious goals set out in the SDGs, we must prioritize and accelerate Climate adaptation and resilience (A&R) efforts.

Protecting People, Economies and Nature

Climate hazards, combined with limited economic resources, leave communities in many parts of the world vulnerable to droughts, floods, and heat stress. Countries and communities in the developing world face the harshest impacts of Climate Change. In sub-Saharan Africa, a warming planet has the potential to increase hunger and food insecurity. In Southeast Asia, coastal cities and communities face increasing risk of severe storms, coastal flooding, and sea level rise that impact lives, economies, and trade. And in certain regions in India, like Bihar and Uttar Pradesh, increased climate risks such as heat waves lead to risks of water scarcity and crop failures.

A&R efforts that protect people, economies, and nature can mitigate these impacts. Consider the ongoing work in a major West African state that is home to more than 20 million people. The government there, has evaluated the potential impact of climate hazards and the actions required to address them. The work revealed impacts to:

- Food. Loss of local crops could threaten food security, requiring importation of 78% of the region's food.

- Health. Up to 400 health centers could be disrupted, affecting more than 2 million patients. In some scenarios, 20,000 people could suffer heat-related deaths – and almost one-third would be children.

- Education. Some 500 schools and Education centers could be inundated, disrupting the learning process of more than 500,000 students.

- Natural Ecosystems. Up to 82% of the state's undeveloped wetlands could face potential loss in biodiversity and ecosystem services by 2050.

In this case, smart and targeted A&R measures would cost about $10 billion while preventing $30 billion in economic damages – a return of 3x.

With insights such as this, the state is shaping an adaptation program with a portfolio of projects that yield the highest impact with limited resources. This includes coastal protection in the most vulnerable areas, wetland restoration, early warning systems, and urban cooling interventions with green spaces.

We believe there are similar potential benefits to A&R action in many other regions and countries. In locations such as Southeast Asia and South Asia, the cost of restoration and disaster response is several times more than the cost of prevention and protection. Simply put, the fallout from not investing in adaptation may make it two to three times harder for us to achieve the SDGs.

Power SDG Progress Through A&R

Decisions on A&R need to be based on the estimated socioeconomic return of those investments – meaning the expected benefits versus the true costs of inaction.

To make sound judgements about the socioeconomic ROI, decision makers must draw on climate science and granular data. They must also have access to financing and funding, innovation, and new technologies. Implementation of A&R plans must then be locally led and fit the local context. And the public sector, private sector, and local community groups must collaborate to implement A&R solutions that are fit for purpose and implemented where they are most needed. Such an approach can allocate scarce resources where they will do the best.

We see encouraging examples of forward-looking governments taking this approach. An East African government developed impact modeling and a response strategy for drought, including identifying vulnerable populations affected and estimating the cost of inaction on poverty levels, hunger, public health, and access to water and sanitation. The insights were used to prioritize the investments needed, including in the food supply chain and insurance interventions for local farmers.

The right investments in adaptation and resilience can channel resources, funding, and technical capacity to where they are needed most.

Similarly, a country in Southeast Asia has conducted a climate-hazard risk assessment for a coastal region prone to flooding, extreme storms, and sea level rise. That assessment has helped the government identify the measures that will have the highest impact in protecting vulnerable people living in poverty near the coast—while also ensuring the stability of the local health care system, local industry and jobs, the agricultural sector, and natural ecosystems such as wetlands.

These examples underscore how the right investments in adaptation and resilience can channel resources, funding, and technical capacity to where they are needed most. If we make A&R a Global priority, we can raise the odds of success in achieving the SDGs.

3. Mobilizing the Private Sector for Sustainability

It will be impossible to achieve the UN's Sustainable Development Goals without bringing the full power of the private sector to bear. Companies across industries and regions have been pushing to make their businesses more sustainable — essentially focusing on the "E" and the "S" in environmental, social, and governance (ESG) topics. And government policy — including new reporting requirements in Europe and the Inflation Reduction Act in the US — are creating even greater momentum.

Yet when it comes to private-sector actions that advance the SDGs, we are not moving nearly fast or far enough today. Companies must supercharge their efforts. This does not mean simply taking on more charitable endeavors. Rather, they need to target areas that enhance their competitive strengths, where they can make a meaningful difference.

The Win-Win

Research, demonstrates that companies achieving meaningful progress on ESG factors earn higher valuation multiples and revenues and have a lower cost of capital.

These findings reflect that sustainable businesses are often better positioned to seize new opportunities and mitigate risks than their rivals.

We see evidence of this across sectors and regions:

- Expanding Markets. There is an often-cited "say-do" gap between consumers' professed interest in sustainable products and their willingness to pay a premium for green products. According to research, however, smart design, marketing, and customer engagement approaches that address the issues that block consumers from choosing sustainable offerings can allow companies to significantly expand their markets.

- Bolstering the Bottom Line. For many companies, reducing emissions is actually an opportunity to improve financial performance, especially in light of recent incentive efforts in the US and the EU. Analysis shows that US automakers that take full advantage of the Inflation Reduction Act could lower their cost of abatement to zero, while pharmaceutical companies could reduce theirs by an average of 77%.

- Building the Brand and Talent. Companies that lead on sustainability, including using their core business to address critical societal challenges and fostering an inclusive culture, are better able to attract and retain the right talent. Analysis shows that 40% of job seekers say they consider a company's sustainability when evaluating job offers.

- Minimizing the Risk of Scarcities. As company sustainability commitments grow, there is a risk that certain resources required to deliver on those promises — everything from minerals required for battery manufacturing to people with the skills to operate climate-smart farms — will be in short supply. Consider that 40%

of Fortune 2000 companies have set net zero targets, but only 2.5% of their suppliers have. The result is likely to be scarcities for critical inputs. Advantage will accrue to those players that move quickly to line up supplies of these resources and, on the flip side, to those that figure out a way to fill the gap.

- Getting Ahead of Government Intervention. Businesses face a rising tide of ESG-related policies and regulations. Countries representing 90% of Global GDP are now aligned to net zero by midcentury, and the number of climate laws has risen twentyfold in the past 25 years. The pace is picking up as governments look to both decarbonize their economies and win a share of the Global green economy—exemplified by the Inflation Reduction Act and the EU's Green Deal Industrial Plan. Far-sighted first movers can get ahead of regulation and position themselves to benefit from the subsidies and investment opportunities available.

The Next Level of Company Action

Companies have a major opportunity to be catalysts for the renewal of energy and effort around the SDGs. Many have already done the hard work of understanding where they can have impact—where they have the core strengths and capabilities to make a difference and where progress could create a material positive impact on their business performance.

Progress on the SDGs will Depend on Unprecedented Levels of Collaboration.

For a food manufacturer, this may involve supporting smallholder farmers to earn a living wage, an action that can not only reduce poverty but also diversify the supply chain and make it more resilient. For an industrial company, meanwhile, efforts to reduce greenhouse gas emissions – including adopting renewable energy, driving energy efficiency, and embracing circularity to reduce raw material consumption – can cut costs significantly.

While companies may understand these opportunities, they must now accelerate their timelines for action. In many cases they cannot do this alone. Progress will depend on unprecedented levels of collaboration – with partners in their supply and value chains, with NGOs, and with governments.

Now is the time for companies to double down on action – both to strengthen competitive advantage and performance and to build a more sustainable and inclusive world.

4. Closing the SDG Financing Gap Requires Collective Creativity

Billions of dollars have been mobilized to advance the Sustainable Development Goals – but it's not news that we need trillions. Estimates put the gap at $3.9 trillion annually. More than mobilizing the capital, we need to put it to work with speed and impact.

That will require creativity and collective resolve across the entire financial ecosystem – from philanthropists to institutional investors, from donor agencies to multilateral development banks (MDBs). And it's possible.

At the risk of oversimplifying, there are three critical areas for action. First, we must expand the use of blended finance models to attract and mobilize private capital. Second, players across the investment ecosystem need to get creative, trying new approaches for accelerating investments. And third, the International financial community must address the high levels of debt facing many developing countries.

Expand Blended Finance

The private sector is the single largest source of capital for advancing the SDGs. But capital from institutional investors, such as pension funds and sovereign wealth funds, is stymied by the real and perceived risks associated with projects in emerging markets and developing economies. Official sources of finance from the MDBs and other development finance institutions (DFIs) can help mitigate these risks and unlock significantly larger flows.

Blended finance is a powerful means of sparking more private-sector investment. Under such arrangements, capital from public sources is invested alongside private capital, with the former serving as a catalyst by lowering risks, lowering costs, and bringing confidence to specific opportunities. Philanthropic capital can play a similar role in absorbing risks and lowering costs – and thus helping to mobilize private capital.

Blended finance is a powerful means of sparking more private-sector investment.

We need more catalytic capital. Fortunately, there are many ways to make that happen. Philanthropies can step up to take first-loss positions. DFIs, such as the International Finance Corporation, can invite even more private capital into their transactions, thereby expanding the pie and mitigating the perceived political risks of good deals. They could even consider syndicating loans to private and institutional investors.

Expanding the provision and scale of political risk insurance from the US International Development Finance Corporation or the Multilateral Investment Guarantee Association could further bolster confidence and significantly scale up the mobilization of private capital.

To make this happen, these institutions must not only shift financial models; they must also shift mindsets. That means revamping delivery models, internal incentives, and processes.

Get Creative Ramping up proven investment approaches won't be enough, however. The Global investment community must also explore completely new ways to accelerate the flow of capital.

There are signs this is beginning to happen. The UN Secretary General, for example, has called for a $500 billion annual "SDG Stimulus." Part of the proposal advocates for using Special Drawing Rights (SDRs), an International reserve issued by the International Monetary Fund. In 2021, approximately $650 billion in SDRs were issued by the IMF, of which just $40 billion or so "belong" to developing economies. The vast majority is held in the reserve accounts of advanced economies.

These reserves may be channeled to MDBs working to drive progress on the Sustainable Development Goals. Presently, efforts are underway at the African Development Bank to make such a channeling of SDRs work. That would provide a major boost to financial capacity and capital for the development agenda across the continent. Making this a reality, however, requires resolve and political will among the world's large economies.

The Global investment community must explore new ways to accelerate the flow of capital.

Local currency financing is another critical area that's ripe for creativity. It's more and more challenging for countries to borrow in dollars, euros, or yuan, despite generating income in their local currencies. Developing new foreign exchange mechanisms that would smooth risks and enable local currency lending will prove instrumental.

Address Debt in the Developing World

Many countries in the developing world are grappling with unsustainable levels of public debt. This limits their ability to invest in the SDGs using domestic resources and curtails their ability to take on new debt, even from concessional sources.

In 2020, many highly indebted countries grappling with the Global pandemic benefitted from the G20's Debt Service Suspension Initiative, which provided a financial lifeline and represented an important example of Global collective action. The G20's Common Framework for Debt Treatments, which followed the debt suspension initiative, now needs to be reworked to incorporate all forms of debt, including all official and private debtors. This will be an unparalleled unlock for financing to flow to emerging markets.

Unless we tackle the challenges of debt distress, we will not be able to free up fiscal space for investment in the SDGs and additional climate initiatives.

The Sustainable Development Goals set out a vision of a sustainable and equitable world. If we are to come close to achieving those goals, we need to bring new energy and creativity to unleashing the necessary capital. This will be possible only if we take collective action that leverages partnerships between the Global North and the Global South and between public institutions and private enterprises. It must go beyond traditional profit motives to aim for real progress and true Global impact.

5. Rethinking Collaboration to Power SDG Progress.

It is a deceptively simple idea: Collaboration is key to achieving the UN'S Sustainable Development Goals. The issues involved — including poverty, Education, and health care — are complex, after all, and require action by multiple stakeholders. And yet despite significant cooperation in some areas, progress is frustratingly slow. That's because while we know collaboration is vital, we don't always collaborate in the most effective ways.

Collaboration focused at the community or regional levels can make it difficult to achieve sufficient scale in a reasonable amount of time. On the flip side, efforts that are too ambitious — say, taking aim at solving problems across all of sub-Saharan Africa — may not gain traction on the ground, the result of too broad a focus and the difficulty of addressing regional nuances. To maximize impact, country-level collaboration is the sweet spot.

In-country collaborations — wherein public-, private-, and social-sector players work together to tackle critical problems — offer three powerful benefits.

First, they encourage the pooling of resources — especially financial resources — from a variety of groups, which in turn enables bigger ambitions and amplified impact. Second, they allow knowledge sharing, ensuring that various participants can bring their expertise to bear on challenges and help strengthen outcomes. And third, collaboration ensures that different organizations and initiatives aren't duplicating efforts.

The Call to Action

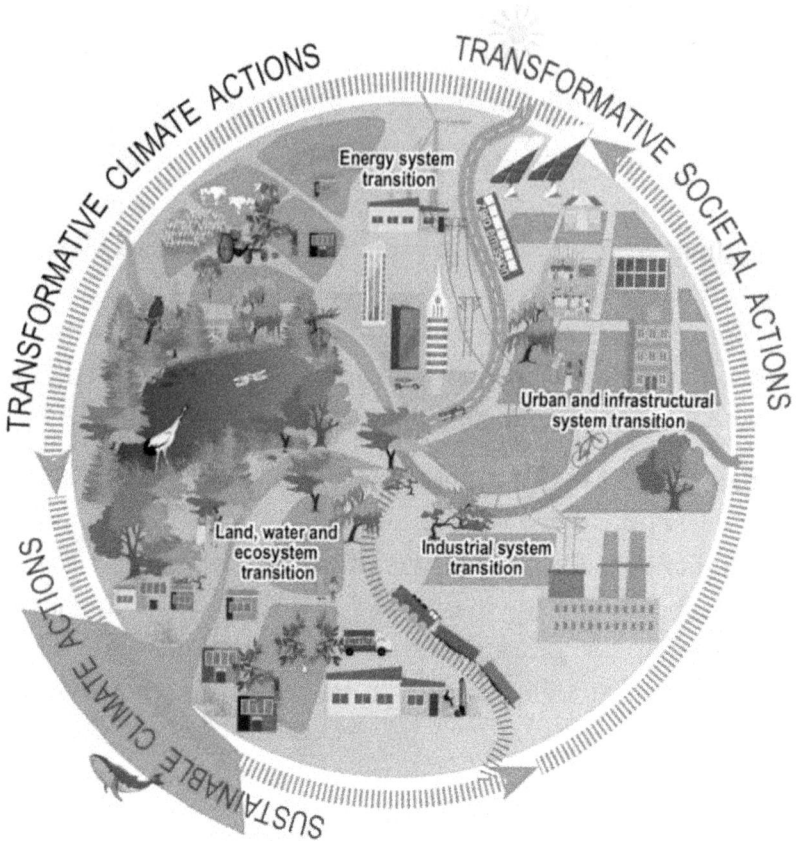

The world is at a crossroads, facing existential threats such as the climate and nature crisis, pandemics, nuclear weapons and artificial intelligence. Among these existential threats, escalating Global conflicts further jeopardise our collective security and stability. These challenges do not belong to one generation; they affect us all.

A Global survey of over 10,000 people of all ages reveals some powerful messages. 76% agree that Climate Change is our greatest threat, and 77% believe leadership must be shared across generations. The message is clear: we need leaders who think beyond short-term goals and take action for a future that benefits everyone. Leaders who respect the rule of law and the independence of the judiciary, support initiatives that strengthen social bonds, combating isolation and discrimination across all demographics. The Summit of the Future offers a crucial platform for this intergenerational dialogue to address our shared challenges. In this pivotal moment of Earth's story, we must provide an opportunity for all countries to share their unique perspectives, collectively shaping a better tomorrow. Only by standing together can we secure a future for generations to come.

Below are a few questions which organizations need to keep in mind -Developing, measuring, implementing and/or oversight of sustainability reporting strategies/technologies?

- Level to which the sustainability reporting processes are embedded within various functions in your organization?

- What level does your company report its Scope 1, 2 and 3 GHG emissions? (Select from dropdown the response?

- How confident are you in your company's ability to measure and report its true GHG emissions?

- Is your organization planning to invest in tools/technologies to facilitate CSRD reporting?

- What types of tools is your organization planning to implement to facilitate CSRD implementation?

- How do you expect the investments related sustainability reporting and data management to change in the next 3 years?

- Are you using AI technologies for supporting sustainability reporting and data management in your organization?

What is the Cost of Climate Inaction?

Economic costs from climate impacts have doubled in the past 20 years.

Without bold climate action, Climate Change will continue to have severe effects on the Global economy:

Companies could lose up to 7% of annual earnings by 2035, with potential asset losses reaching $560–610 billion annually, particularly in the telecommunications, utilities, and energy sectors.

But here is the good news: Climate leadership pays off.

By committing to decarbonization, climate adaptation, the private sector can navigate climate risks and unlock vast long-term benefits.

For example, businesses already investing in these areas are seeing returns of up to $19 for every dollar spent.

"Climate Change has traditionally been characterised as an environmental issue...this is a fundamental misperception. Rather, Climate Change is the ultimate sustainable development issue [...] The Climate Change we face today arises from the accumulated results of two centuries of unsustainable development in industry, energy production, land use, lifestyles, and consumption patterns."

A big part of tackling Climate Change is making sure countries around the world can develop in a sustainable manner, so that people can prosper and enjoy good living standards without harming the planet!

Four concrete principles that societies can use to design and build alternative sustainable ways of living.

These principles are:

- Do not allow mined materials to increase in use or waste.

- Do not allow synthetic compounds to increase in use or waste.

- Do not destroy nature or remove natural systems.

- Do not erode or undermine people's ability to meet their own basic needs.

Once Climate Change becomes a clear and present danger to financial stability, it could already be too late to stabilise the atmosphere at two degrees." What is being emphasised is the huge financial risks that stem from only viewing the short-term. Climate Change will impact our economies if we don't take a longer view and recognise that it requires us to change how we currently do things.

Let's have a look at some specific examples of these impacts on UK businesses and the country's economy. An increase in flooding from sea levels rising and changes to rainfall patterns due to Climate Change are serious concerns in the UK. Every year, floods cause an estimated 800 million pounds of damage to non-residential properties. This could rise by 25 percent to 1 billion pounds by 2050.

Another big problem for businesses related to Climate Change is the rise in temperature and especially extreme heat. For example, the heat wave which struck in 2003 cost UK businesses between 400 and 500 million pounds as infrastructure was damaged, people couldn't go to their workplaces, and in general, it was hard to move goods around. What's more, over 2000 people died in the UK. Such heatwaves are expected to occur more often in the future.

Climate Change is a consequence of living in an unsustainable manner. It undermines three key strands of life: economic, social, and environmental. When it comes to Climate Change, cheap is expensive. Tackling Climate Change now and moving to a low carbon economy will be cheaper than dealing with its consequences.

Have you, your family or friends already experienced any of the impacts of Climate Change? For example, extreme weather like storms or floods? And what about droughts or wildfires? Or maybe pollution from excess burning of fossil fuels? The impacts of Climate Change are happening now. And action is needed right now if we want to make a positive difference to improve the health of the planet for the future.

Sustainable businesses can employ a three-pronged strategy:

1. Preserve the environment and conserve natural resources.
2. Build social equity, support employee well-being and promote fair trade.
3. Maximize long-term profitability and promote growth.

This holistic view of doing business places equal emphasis on the planet, people and profit. You'll often see the concept referred to as the triple bottom line.

Overarching Considerations for the Future

As countries across the world work their way out of a devastating pandemic, there is a unique opportunity to make a strong push towards a green recovery that marks the beginning of low- carbon, resource and energy efficient, nature positive, job-rich and socially inclusive growth. This is potentially a transformational moment after decades of reliance on fossil fuel-driven production and consumption.

While intentionality matters, the road to a green recovery will not be even and it will challenge most economies, especially those with limited fiscal space and heavy debt burdens.

The scale, impact and depth of the Triple Planetary Crisis will necessitate a range of solutions that combine fixing the upstream macroeconomic enabling environment and downstream projects that restore and build degraded environments and ecosystems.

Solutions will need to be tailored and will depend on contextual realities, including the extent of environmental degradation and a whole host of other transition imperatives related to finance, capacity, leadership, knowledge infrastructure, technologies, and other inputs so critical to forward momentum. While knowledge gaps remain, enough is already known to warrant bold action for comprehensive, integrated approaches to mitigation and adaptation.

Balancing Development, Mitigation, and Adaptation:

As industries embark on decarbonization, their ability to make good on their COP pledges will largely depend on three factors: Policy, technological innovation, the pace at which carbon-intensive "brown" businesses can be converted into greener ones, and the deployment of massive waves of new capital.

What is ESG reporting?

ESG has seen a meteoric rise in prominence for investors, employees, and businesses alike. But what is ESG and why does it matter to a business's performance? ESG is an acronym that stands for Environmental, Social, and Governance. It is a framework used to measure a business's non-financial performance in environmental, social and governance categories. ESG was coined in 2004 by former UN Secretary-General Kofi Annan, resulting in 2005 with the first study, "Who cares Wins" developed jointly with the world's largest institutional investors.

Why is ESG Important for Businesses?

Across the EU and the UK, key ESG reporting regulations, such as the Corporate Sustainability Reporting Directive (CSRD) cover more than 75% of European companies' turnover. ESG has become an important way for investors, consumers, and potential employees to access the attractiveness and sustainability of a business.

"ESG is likely to play a bigger role in how companies are assessed, not only by investors but by consumers and stakeholders". "The numbers reflect a growing awareness that companies must manage their environmental impact in innovative ways to remain successful. Sustainability is the new ideal, and the development of sophisticated   methods of evaluating ESG activities and effect, is the key to attaining it," he adds. An extensive suite of reporting templates and tools to bring your business's ESG reporting to the next level.

What are the Key Pillars of ESG?

- ✓ **Environmental (E) Pillar:** an organization's environmental impact, incl. its efforts to reduce carbon emissions, conserve resources & minimize pollution.

- ✓ **Social (S) Pillar:** an organization's relationships with its stakeholders, incl. employees, communities, customers & suppliers, as well as its commitment to diversity, equity & inclusion.

- ✓ **Governance (G) Pillar:** the mechanisms & processes through which organizations are directed & controlled, incl. board oversight, transparency, ethical conduct & risk management.

ESG Is More Than Just a Collection of Buzzwords

Taken together, the 3 pillars of ESG represent a holistic approach to business that recognizes that companies do not just exist to make a profit: they also have a responsibility to their stakeholders & to society at large. Let us take a few examples!

- ✓ **Environmental (E) Pillar:** Businesses that pay attention to their carbon footprint & work to reduce their impact on the environment are not just helping the planet but they are also positioning themselves to succeed in a world where Climate Change is an increasingly urgent issue. Consumers & investors alike are demanding that companies take Climate Change seriously, and businesses that do not, risk losing out in the long term.

- ✓ **Social (S) Pillar:** Businesses do not operate in a vacuum. Companies that are good to their employees, treat their suppliers fairly, engage with the communities where they operate will be better positioned to succeed in the long term. A strong social commitment to diversity, equity & inclusion is also essential in today's increasingly diverse & interconnected world.

✓ **Governance (G) Pillar:** This pillar ensures that companies are being held to high ethical standards. When companies have transparent governance processes for decision-making & oversight, they are less likely to engage in practices that could harm their stakeholders (employees, customers, society at large, etc.).

ESG has become increasingly important in the business world. **Companies that prioritize the ESG principles are likely to be the ones that thrive in the years to come.**

Chapter 5

How does ESG Add Value to Businesses?

ESG Wheel:
Key Themes and Topics

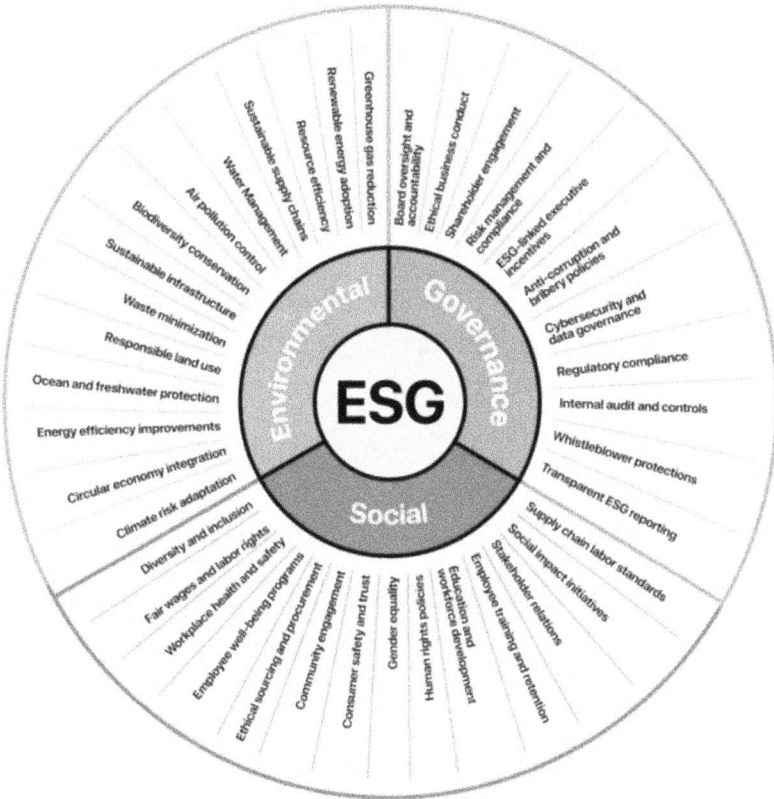

ESG has become an integral part of assessing a company's value. It has been demonstrated that companies performing well on ESG practices have higher financial growth and optimisation,

lower volatility, higher employee productivity, reduced regulatory and legal interventions (fines and sanctions), top-line growth, and cost reductions. On the other hand, companies that performed poorly on ESG noticed a higher cost of capital, higher volatility due to controversies and other incidences such as labour strikes, fraud accounting and other governance irregularities.

There are clear advantages to optimising ESG performance, such as:

- High ESG performance makes your company more attractive to VCs and other private equity investors.

- Integrating ESG gives you a clear competitive advantage. Studies have found that 88% of companies that adhered to social and environmental standards showed better operational development.

- ESG optimisation allows you to get ahead of the curve and be prepared for upcoming reporting and regulation requirements.

- ESG reporting gives you clarity on your business's impact and allows you to avoid greenwashing and the negative PR that can come from it. It is no longer acceptable to make unsubstantiated sustainability claims, and businesses risk their reputations if they do not have an integrated ESG strategy.

- High ESG scores allow you to attract and retain the best

talent. 67% of millennials expect the companies they work for to be purpose-driven and their jobs to have a societal impact.

What is ESG Measuring?

ESG stands for Environmental, Social and Governance and is an important, if still emerging, framework for measuring a company's non-financial performance. Before the onset of ESG reporting, financial reporting and capital dominated how investors measure company performance. But in an era marked by Climate Change, investors, consumers, employees, and business owners alike are looking for more comprehensive and inclusive ways of measuring a company's performance and impact.

What are the Three Pillars of ESG? E: Environmental

The Environmental pillar considers the impact a business has on the planet. Top of mind in this category is a company's record on climate, its greenhouse gas emissions and overall carbon footprint. Measures such as accurate and up-to-date carbon accounting, reporting, and decarbonisation plans are critical in this area.

But the E in ESG does not stop at a company's climate impacts. Other considerations to measure and account for are water pollution, water use, and air pollution. In addition, business report on land use practices that affect deforestation and biodiversity in this category. Finally, a company's recycling policy and whether or not it has a circular economic model also impact its score.

The E in ESG is the most complex to gather data on, particularly as up to 90% of a company's emissions can be attributed to Scope

3 emissions, which can be challenging to report.

The Social pillar in ESG reports on a company's human impact, from its employees and consumers to the communities within which a company operates. Employee and labour practices, health and safety standards, mental health, customer success, and community relations are all reported in this category. Companies also report on issues of equity, including gender and diversity inclusion. Customer success, including product liabilities "regarding the safety and quality of their product," is also considered.

G: Governance

Governance deals with a company's leadership, executive pay, audits, internal controls, and shareholder rights. Investors want to know if they can trust the company and what kind of decisions are taken behind closed doors. Some factors that could impact an organisation's Governance score are the makeup of the board of directors, executive compensation guidelines, political contributions and lobbying, and hiring and onboarding best practices.

Who is Looking at ESG Scores?

The rise of ESG reflects a growing appetite among investors, consumers, employees, and business owners for a more sustainable and ethical way of doing business. The ever-increasing interest in measuring and ranking ESG by firms and investors reflects the perspective that environmental, social, and governance dimensions should be factored in when considering business success.

What is ESG Reporting Software?

ESG software is a powerful tool that allows businesses to enter data, track performance, and generate reports on their non-financial performance. Some data points that could be included in ESG reporting are greenhouse gas emissions, waste production, water usage, governance structure, employee satisfaction, board representation, and diversity, equity and inclusion.

What are the Benefits of Using ESG Reporting Software?

ESG software enables businesses to pull reports, track their performance, and set targets. ESG software also provides a measure of quality assurance and is an important part of standardising ESG reporting across sectors. Finally, ESG software provides businesses with essential insight and empowers them to make the most effective and data-driven decisions to become more sustainable.

Streamline ESG reporting tools to help optimise your business's performance and get you ahead of the pack on ESG. ESG templates allows you to create and send questionnaires to report ESG-related and non-financial dimensions. As a result, any Sustainability Manager can now cover all internal and external ESG reporting needs, adapting to any framework in a few clicks.

What are challenges to ESG reporting that businesses should consider?

Investors increasingly view ESG scores as essential signifiers of a company's robustness and sustainability. While ESG becomes an increasingly important measure of company performance, there are several caveats and challenges this emerging field must consider.

To live up to its promise, ESG will need to increase transparency and accountability in data collection and reporting and scale up knowledge and capacity within businesses.

1. **Lack of Capacity**

First, there is the question of businesses' capacity and ability to keep up with reporting requirements. Studies have found that many companies are unprepared to gather and report their ESG data. For instance, more than half of businesses are housing their ESG data in spreadsheets instead of using ESG reporting software.

2. **Lack of Data Collection Standards**

Second, a lack of clarity around what data needs to be collected and reported makes it difficult to compare scores across and within sectors. "This is the biggest challenge facing sustainable investing: there is no clear-cut criteria about what makes a company ESG investable,". "That is another reason why we so definitely need the data quality,". "As long as you don't have robust methodologies, there is no policing of what is qualifying as ESG investment".

This lack of clarity and transparency around ESG reporting can lead to accusations of greenwashing, which is increasingly a liability for businesses.

How does the EU Support Standards in ESG Reporting?

A Model for the world to follow.

The EU has been ramping up reporting regulations and frameworks to add teeth to ESG reporting, making it much harder for businesses to get away with unsubstantiated and misleading claims about sustainability. For instance, the EU is soon set to tighten ESG disclosure requirements for large businesses.

According to a press release by the European Council, the EU has agreed on plans to mandate large businesses to disclose more information relating to their environmental, social and governance (ESG) plans and performance from January 2024 onwards. Companies will need to disclose the impacts of their activities and supply chains on people and the environment.

This is fantastic news for consumers and the planet. Greenwashing distracts from the work that needs to be done and gives consumers a false sense of security that their choices are indeed earth-friendly. According to Bruno Le Maire, the new mandate on ESG reporting "is excellent news for all European consumers. They will now be better informed about the impact of business on human rights and the environment."

The Global economy has a long way to go regarding accountability, but this new mandate is a step in the right direction.

What is the Future of ESG?

Underlying the new focus on ESG reports is the understanding that more factors than financial performance affect a company's performance and sustainability. Consumers partly drive the increasing importance of ESG, 80% of which agree that a business must play a role in addressing societal issues; they want a company to take actions which increase profits, improve social conditions, and make the world a better place."

Investor preference is also driving the rise of ESG. Indeed, studies have shown that 49% of millennial millionaires make their investments based on social factors.

And finally, corporations are interested in optimising ESG performance to stay ahead of regulations and competitors. Studies have found that some 63% of sustainable funds performed in the top half of their respective categories in 2018.

ESG is increasingly the model for non-financial reporting and regulations, such as the EU Taxonomy, the Sustainable Finance Disclosure Regulation (SFDR), and as well as the entity-level disclosure for reporting on the EU's Sustainable Finance Related Disclosure (SFRD).

The rapid rise in ESG reporting requirements has been a challenge for many businesses. A survey of business leaders from the US and UK found that "more than 90% see ESG issues as a financial imperative but that 79% are unprepared to meet the proposed reporting requirements".

Is ESG reporting right for my business?

High ESG performance makes your company more attractive to VCs and other private equity investors.

- Integrating ESG gives you a clear competitive advantage.
- ESG optimisation allows you to get ahead of the curve and be prepared for upcoming reporting and regulation requirements.
- ESG reporting gives you clarity on your business's impact and allows you to avoid greenwashing and the negative PR that can come from it.
- High ESG scores allow you to attract and retain the best talent.
- Business with high ESG performances is more competitive.

We hope this overview of ESG has been helpful and inspired you to either integrate these criteria into your business practices or take your existing ESG practices to a new level. Helping companies optimise their ESG performance, reduce their negative impact on the planet, and decarbonise their operations.

Definitions of Corporate Sustainability

The definition of a sustainable business varies depending on the field. For example:

- In agribusiness, corporate sustainability can encompass concepts such as organic farming, urban horticulture and permaculture.

- In manufacturing, sustainability efforts may include waste elimination, greenhouse gas reduction, finding the most efficient and profitable use of existing resources (such as oil, gas, ores and forests) and creating energy-efficient infrastructures.

- In retail, sustainability experts often focus on the supply chain, evaluating ways to minimize waste in packaging, facilitate energy use in stores, transport goods in more

- eco-friendly ways and recycle old products.

Corporate sustainability also has a strong social component. Factors like leadership diversity, equitable CEO-to-average worker pay ratio and low employee turnover all play an important part in sustainability rankings.

Benefits of Sustainable Business

In addition to saving the planet, sustainable practices generate a number of benefits. These practices help a company:

- **Save Money:** Employing eco-friendly technologies and cutting down on waste in energy, resources and employee time generates significant annual savings. Even simple steps like turning off computer monitors can have an effect.

- **Boost Market Share:** Lean, efficient businesses with a reputation for earth-friendly profits now attract a lot of attention from savvy investors, new customers and the press. Investors, in particular, like to see that cost-saving measures are in place.

- **Create Green-Collar Jobs:** Thanks to an increasing focus on sustainability, a lot of new titles have been introduced into our lexicon, including passive solar building designer, wind energy engineer and energy-efficient construction worker. Some believe that renewable energy development could create millions of new jobs.

- **Attract and Retain Employees:** Businesses with fair and ethical practices are like catnip to highly qualified employees. Happier workers also tend to perform better, circumventing the expensive process of firing and rehiring.

Who Is Affected by Climate Change?

When we talk about Climate Change, people often think of melting ice and polar bears. Yes, ice is melting but that's not the only climate impact, as you've learned. Climate Change affects people too! Mostly, people who are already vulnerable and discriminated against.

Carbon Dioxide Emissions Around the Globe

Climate Change is also a justice issue because the ones who suffer the most from climate impacts are the ones who have contributed the least toward the problem.

This is true Globally, where developing countries have contributed very little toward greenhouse gas emissions in the past, but are being hit with the most severe impacts. This is also true about future generations, who have hardly contributed to the climate problem, but experience the consequences.

Three Key Observations

This leads us to the concept of climate justice, which contains three key observations:

1. The ones who contributed the least to Climate Change often suffer the most from climate impacts.

2. Marginalised communities are the most vulnerable to climate impacts.

3. Our present generations have a duty to act.

Climate justice raises questions that don't have an easy answer. It's difficult to determine what works for people in different parts of the world.

For Example:

- Who is creating the most emissions and who should cut the most in present day terms?

- Who historically created the most emissions, and how does that affect cuts that should be made in the future?

Hopefully, you agree that tackling Climate Change is the right thing to do. There are four imperatives underpinning our need to take action: personal, moral, legal, and economic.

These four imperatives clearly show that acting on Climate Change is the right thing to do: it makes moral, legal and economic sense.

Bold Action for a Resilient Future

Business leaders should be in direct dialogue with their peers from higher Education, government and civil society with a focus on radically accelerating shared sustainability goals through collaborative leadership and systems change. Through inspiring thought leadership, experts can facilitate the exchange of ideas, openly discuss bold strategies and confront the most pressing challenges faced by leaders today, providing organisations with solutions for short-term challenges and paths to reach long-term goals.

In today's rapidly evolving business landscape, integrating Environmental, Social, and Governance (ESG) principles isn't just a trend; it's a pathway toward creating lasting value and resilience. Aligning ESG goals with the United Nations Sustainable Development Goals (SDGs) helps organizations address Global challenges while achieving business objectives.

Why Aligning ESG with SDGs Matters

The big question, then, is how do ESG and SDGs connect

Simply put, the SDGs provide the Global goals, and ESG provides the business framework to meet those goals. By aligning ESG practices with the SDGs, businesses can ensure that their actions contribute not only to their internal success but also to broader, Globally recognized targets.

For instance An ESG strategy focused on reducing carbon emissions directly aligns with SDG 13: Climate Action.

- A governance strategy that prioritizes transparency and anti-corruption aligns with SDG 16: Peace, Justice, and Strong Institutions.

- Social strategies that emphasize diversity and inclusion contribute to SDG 10: Reduced Inequalities.

The SDGs offer businesses a common language and Global targets to work toward, ensuring that individual business actions collectively contribute to the larger sustainability transition. By integrating the SDGs into their ESG strategies, companies can align their operational objectives with Global sustainability goals, driving meaningful impact while enhancing their long-term resilience.

ESG Metrics & KPIs – Are You Measuring What Matters?

Tracking ESG performance is about way more than compliance — it's about driving real impact.

Without clear Key Performance Indicators (KPIs), progress remains unclear, and stakeholder trust is harder to build.

It reinforces the importance of structured measurement across Environmental, Social, and Governance dimensions.

Environmental: Metrics like energy efficiency improvements, waste recycling rates, and carbon intensity provide tangible insights into sustainability performance.

Social: Tracking gender representation, employee satisfaction, and community investment fosters inclusivity and well-being.

Governance: Board diversity, anti-corruption cases, and ESG-linked executive compensation ensure transparency and accountability.

Why It Matters:

Robust ESG KPIs drive meaningful change, ensure regulatory compliance, and build trust with investors, customers, and employees. Transparency and accountability are not just buzzwords — they define the future of sustainable business.

How is your organization measuring sustainability?

ESG Risks and Opportunities

The foundations upon which modern-day ESG will be built, how market forces react to ESG, and ways to create and maintain value using ESG investment strategies.

The five pathways of materiality, and how they can interplay with or against ESG performance.

The many challenges that corporations face when it comes to leveraging ESG investing into their portfolios, and how the changing landscape of ESG is making this an area of untapped potential when it comes to the financial workings of businesses today. From real-life case studies you can assess risk, create better risk management policy, and build a map to identify valuable areas of opportunity and create better decision-making approaches. A look at portfolio optimization and the utilization of ESG factors to maximize returns in addition to examining different funds and how investors can blend ESG into their investment portfolio.

Create the best framework of a solid risk management plan using smarter methods to identify risk, navigate ESG issues, and reach

ESG investing goals.

ESG and Climate Change

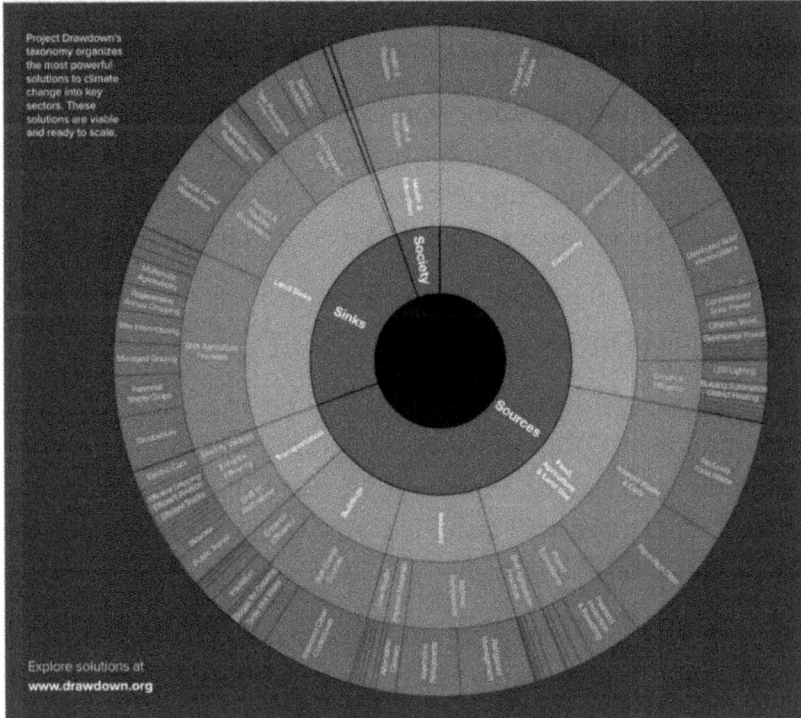

Focus on understanding Climate Change and the risks and opportunities that it creates for businesses in the 21st century. Analyse the current impacts of Climate Change on a Global scale, and the investment shifts that are required to achieve a net-zero economy. Also analyze the role of climate disclosures and their importance in ESG.

Review private environmental governance, the active role that private companies are playing in combating Climate Change, and the parallels between the public and private sectors. Also assess the insurance industry and the ways that it spreads risk, as well as creative ways that insurance as a form of private or public governance can build climate resilience. Review the concept of greenwashing: what is driving firms to make exaggerated environmental claims, why it is harmful, and examples of enforcement actions.

A thorough understanding of public and private environmental governance, the financial risks that unmitigated Climate Change is creating, climate disclosures, and innovative ways that business leaders can view and implement climate solutions is important.

ESG Expert Duties and Skills

The start of this decade has seen more than its share of crises, including the COVID pandemic, a war in Europe and growing economic uncertainty. Although we can't predict when these current challenges will fade, it seems certain that the climate crisis will outlast all of them.

For almost three centuries since the dawn of the industrial revolution, human ingenuity has produced remarkable inventions and unprecedented prosperity for much of the world. But this has come from the use of fossil fuels that have produced carbon emissions at an unsustainable level. Now we must move to a net zero world in which we both seek to eliminate net carbon emissions and expand Global economic opportunity. This will require sweeping changes in every sector of the economy in every country in the world. And we must achieve all this in only three decades.

In the history of civilization, few generations have needed to do as much in as little time as we must do now. At its most fundamental level, this is the single greatest challenge and opportunity of our time.

Closing the Sustainability Skills Gap: Helping businesses move from pledges to progress

CHECKLIST
CHIEF SUSTAINABILITY OFFICER

STRATEGY AND LEADERSHIP

- [ ] Develop Sustainability Vision
- [ ] Align ESG with business
- [ ] Lead sustainability team
- [ ] Champion internal advocacy
- [ ] Portfolio sustainability projects

STAKEHOLDER ENGAGEMENT

- [ ] Map key stakeholders
- [ ] Conduct engagement activities
- [ ] Organize sustainability forusm
- [ ] Drive community initiatives
- [ ] Build investor relations

SUSTAINABILITY REPORTING

- [ ] Publish ESG reports
- [ ] Adhere to GRI/SASB
- [ ] Analyse sustainability metrics
- [ ] Disclose carbon footprint
- [ ] Enhance report transparency

REGULATORY COMPLIANCE

- [ ] Monitor ESG legislation
- [ ] Conduct risk assessments
- [ ] Start compliance measures
- [ ] Advise on ESG risks
- [ ] Update ESG policies

ENVIRONMENTAL INITIATIVES

- [ ] Reduce carbon footprint
- [ ] Enhance energy efficiency
- [ ] Manage waste responsibly
- [ ] Optimise water usage
- [ ] Promote biodiversity projects

SOCIAL RESPONSIBILITY

- [ ] Improve labor practices
- [ ] Enhance community engagement
- [ ] Promote social equity
- [ ] Support employee wellbeing
- [ ] Foster employee volunteerism

ECONOMIC SUSTAINABILITY

- [ ] Guide ESG investing
- [ ] Promote sustainable business
- [ ] Optimise sustainable growth
- [ ] Encourage ethical practices
- [ ] Evaluate ESG performance

PRODUCT DEV & INNOVATION

- [ ] Encourage green innovations
- [ ] Develop eco-friendly products
- [ ] Implement design thinking
- [ ] Foster creative solutions
- [ ] Scouting & Experimenting

SUPPLY CHAIN MANAGEMENT

- [ ] Promote responsible sourcing
- [ ] Evaluate suppliers' sustainability
- [ ] Reduce logistics emissions
- [ ] Implement circular practices
- [ ] Enhance supply chain transparency

ORGANIZATIONAL CAPABILITIES

- [ ] Develop sustainability curriculum
- [ ] Green Skills Training Employees
- [ ] Foster Cultural Change
- [ ] Support sustainability champions
- [ ] Portfolio sustainability projects

PARTNERSHIP & COLLABORATION

- [ ] Initiate ESG partnerships
- [ ] Collaborate on sustainability
- [ ] Engage with NGOs
- [ ] Participate in ESG networks
- [ ] Leverage academic research

MONITORING & EVALUATION

- [ ] Set ESG performance KPIs
- [ ] Monitor sustainability progress
- [ ] Utilise sustainability software
- [ ] Conduct ESG audits
- [ ] Embed sustainability in organization

Like the space age and digital era, the world's sustainability transformation calls not only for a new generation of technology but a new generation of knowledge and skills. Clearly, no single entity can meet this challenge alone. The key will be to partner broadly and effectively with others to move the world's workforce into the future. We know the proposals in this report don't have all the answers, but we believe the world must commit to a Global Sustainability Skilling Strategy based on a concerted and coordinated effort from companies, industry organizations, learning providers and governments.

As companies move to create and fill these jobs, they are confronting a huge sustainability skills gap. This gap encompasses three categories. First, some employees need deep and specialized sustainability knowledge and skills in areas like carbon accounting, carbon removal and ecosystem services valuation. This includes the skills needed to address these issues through new climate-specific digital tools.

Second, broader business teams need readier access to more limited but sometimes deep knowledge in specific sustainability subject areas, such as climate-related issues that have become important for procurement and supply chain management.

Third, a great many employees need basic and broader fluency in sustainability issues and climate science fields that impact a wide variety of business operations and processes.

Ultimately, it's important to recognize that the sustainability transformation will need people who can combine specialized sustainability knowledge and skills with varying degrees of other multidisciplinary skill sets. These will need to combine knowledge from STEM and other fields in the liberal arts and encompass skills that span across business, the use of data, and digital technology. This combination currently is hard to find and often doesn't exist naturally.

Perhaps unsurprisingly, we've also learned that the sustainability skills gap is creating an increasing sense of anxiety for business leaders. This reflects not only the enormity of the climate crisis but two other factors as well.

First, there are growing public expectations that companies will turn their climate pledges into progress. In the next 24 months, regulators in multiple countries will likely require that public companies report their carbon emissions. A great many businesses are not yet equipped with the skilled personnel, business processes and data systems needed for this step. Business leaders understandably fear that, if their reports are incomplete or show a lack of progress, they will confront growing public criticism.

Second, this pressure for performance is growing while economic concerns are rising. Economic turbulence is putting added pressure on companies to find new ways to do more with less. In some instances, companies may even be tempted to postpone or forego new business initiatives, including pursuing their climate pledges.

Yet ongoing scientific observations and data show that the world cannot afford to wait. The United Nations Environment Programme made clear in its annual Emissions Gap report that current National climate plans fall short of what will be needed to meet the world's climate targets.

Clearly the business community will need to do more. Other institutions must as well. Climate pledges and performance are equally important for every organization on the planet, including nonprofits and even government institutions themselves. In short, we're all in this together, and we need to come together to chart a successful path forward, including by investing in sustainability skills.

Yet, today, the gap between sustainability workforce needs and the number of qualified people available is growing. According to the LinkedIn Green Jobs report, green jobs grew at an annual rate of 8% between 2015 and 2021, while the talent pool grew at only 6%.

As these figures reflect, progress is underway, but it's not moving fast enough. To date, most companies at the forefront of sustainability transformation have been scrappy, growing the "home-grown" talent, they need. Our research found that employers so far have tapped 68% of their sustainability leaders by hiring from within their own company. Some 60% of sustainability team members joined without expertise in the field. Employers mostly have tapped talented insiders with the core transformational and functional skill sets needed to create change in a company, even though they lacked formal training in sustainability. They then upskilled those individuals to accomplish critical sustainability work.

The biggest problem with this approach is that it will not scale to meet either the business community's or the planet's needs. As we look at the roughly 3,900 companies that have made climate pledges, it's readily apparent that the work to turn these pledges into progress will require far more talent with sustainability skills and fluency than currently is being trained within these companies' businesses.

How do we Move Further and Faster?

This is a fundamental question, and we offer in this book both some suggestions and a commitment as a company to do more. Progress will be needed in three areas.

First, we all need to work together to develop a shared understanding, based on better data, regarding evolving jobs and the sustainability knowledge and skills needed for them. Currently, data remains spotty. We need a better and common taxonomy and framework that builds on recent sustainability work by International organizations, National governments, and private companies. We believe sustainability skilling can borrow from recent advances to address cybersecurity skilling to help create a better roadmap linking specific sustainability skills, training, jobs and career paths.

Work will be needed from a broad array of stakeholders. To develop a shared understanding of sustainability workforce needs, Microsoft and LinkedIn will support efforts to define skills and competencies and enable the mapping of sustainability skills and jobs as they evolve. We will achieve this in part through partnerships with organizations like the International Labour Organization and our work with the Development Data Partnership, which includes the Organisation for Economic Co-operation and Development (OECD), the World Bank, Inter-American Development Bank (IADB), United Nations Development Programme (UNDP), International Monetary Fund (IMF) and other multilateral organizations.

Second, employers must move quickly to upskill their workforce through learning initiatives focused on sustainability knowledge and skills. This will require support from a variety of learning partners, including Educational institutions, vocational Education providers, apprenticeship programs and online training providers. This work must start with the development of new learning materials that can be used both in person and online. This must be supported by expanded learning initiatives to reach employees in companies and more broadly across the workforce. There is an opportunity for government policy and funding to help scale these efforts.

Third, the world must prepare the next generation of workers for the sustainability jobs of the future. Just as governments, NGOs and companies have worked to bring digital skilling and computer science into schools, we will need similar partnerships to bring sustainability fluency and science into primary and secondary schools. And higher Education institutions will need to strengthen and expand their undergraduate and graduate sustainability programs.

All these efforts can move faster if governments and public-private partnerships develop stronger sustainability programs through country-level networks and centers of excellence, foster International professional forums and communities of practice, and create real-world interdisciplinary learning opportunities for students.

Understanding of the main issues in the field of sustainability and demystifying guidelines for drafting sustainability reports, International principles, and management models in the field of sustainability are the following -

- Defining models and methodologies for measuring economic, social, and environmental impacts.

- Leveraging in-depth knowledge of the ESG landscape to

engage with client stakeholders and capitalise on product Solutioning.

- Track developments in sustainable environmental and social trends, including current and emerging thematic drivers, key players, best practices and the regulatory landscape, etc.

- Building conceptual and technical knowledge on ESG and sustainability (incl. climate risk).

As Sustainability becomes a priority for businesses, the Chief Sustainability Officer plays a central role in driving strategy and implementation. Here are 12 key functions that outline the responsibilities of this position:

1. Strategic Vision & Leadership – Aligning sustainability goals with long-term business objectives.

2. Sustainability Integration – Incorporating sustainability into core operations and decision-making across all departments.

3. Stakeholder Engagement – Engaging with internal and external stakeholders, including investors, customers, and communities.

4. Policy & Regulatory Compliance – Ensuring adherence to current and emerging ESG regulations.

5. Climate Risk Management – Identifying and managing climate-related risks and opportunities.

6. Sustainability Reporting – Overseeing accurate and transparent ESG reporting.

7. Innovation – Leading innovation in sustainable product

development and business models.

8. Partnership Development – Establishing partnerships with NGOs, external organizations, and government bodies.

9. Supply Chain Responsibility – Applying sustainability standards throughout the supply chain.

10. Sustainable Finance – Working with finance teams to integrate sustainability into investment decisions.

11. Employee Engagement & Culture – Building a sustainability-focused culture through training and communication.

12. Performance Monitoring & Metrics – Establishing KPIs and tracking sustainability performance.

The CSO role is crucial in embedding sustainability into the business model, ensuring alignment with strategic goals and regulatory standards.

Top 5 Corporate Sustainability Trends Every Sustainability Professional Should Embrace

Sustainability is gaining traction across organizations worldwide. Integrating Sustainability into the business model not only ensures long-term success but also enhances corporate reputation. Here are the top 5 sustainability trends every professional should embrace to keep their organization ahead:

- **Circular Economy Practices**

  Transition from a linear "take-make-waste" model to a circular one that emphasizes reusing, recycling, and regenerating products and materials. This not only reduces waste but also creates new business opportunities.

- **Climate Action and Carbon Neutrality**

  Commit to reducing greenhouse gas emissions and achieving carbon neutrality. Implement energy-efficient practices, invest in renewable energy sources, and participate in carbon offset programs to make a tangible impact.

- **Sustainable Supply Chain Management**

  Ensure that every link in your supply chain adheres to sustainable practices. This includes ethical sourcing, minimizing environmental impact, and promoting fair labor practices. Transparency and traceability are key.

- **Green Finance and Investment**

  Integrate environmental, social, and governance (ESG) criteria into financial decisions. Support and invest in companies that prioritize sustainability and explore green bonds and sustainable investing options.

- **Employee Engagement**

  Foster a culture of sustainability within your organization by engaging employees and communities. Encourage sustainable practices at work and support local environmental initiatives to create a positive impact beyond the corporate walls.

Understanding these five aspects is essential. By exchanging information and best practices with peers, we can collectively drive progress and innovation in sustainability.

A Unified Approach for Sustainable Success

To succeed in today's sustainability-driven world, businesses must go beyond isolated, one-off actions. They need to align their efforts with both ESG frameworks and the SDGs to ensure they're not just improving their own performance but contributing to the Global agenda for a more sustainable, equitable, and prosperous future.

The bottom line is this: ESG gives businesses the tools, but the SDGs provide the map. Together, they form the core component every sustainability leader must master to future-proof their business and create lasting positive change.

Mapping ESG goals to the SDGs enables companies to communicate their broader contributions to society and the environment. This alignment allows stakeholders, including investors, customers, and employees, to see the tangible impact of corporate sustainability efforts. By demonstrating how ESG actions contribute to Global priorities, companies can reinforce their role as responsible Global citizens, committed to driving both business success and societal progress.

From extreme weather events to shifting regulations, addressing climate resilience isn't only necessary — it's mission critical

- How Climate Change is already disrupting operations and supply chains

- The financial implications of failing to address climate risks

- Key strategies to protect your business and drive growth through sustainability

As Climate Change evolves into a Global crisis, the effects of extreme events such as droughts and floods are not equally distributed. Age, gender, and geographical location impact vulnerability to the negative outcomes associated with climate crises.

As ESG becomes more mainstream, reporting requirements continue to evolve. The field is growing rapidly, which means even if you're new, you're not far behind — everyone needs to keep up. This article will help you understand the basics: What is reporting? What's the difference between voluntary and mandatory disclosures? What purpose do they serve?

Mastering these concepts will boost your chances of securing an ESG role and help you stand out by showing how ESG frameworks influence business strategy.

Sustainability disclosure refers to the process of reporting a company's sustainability performance, covering aspects such as:

- Environmental, social, and governance (ESG) metrics.

- Progress toward sustainability goals

- Risks related to sustainability challenge

These disclosures provide transparency to stakeholders (investors, regulators, customers, etc.) and help them understand how the company is addressing key sustainability issues.

Sustainability disclosure is shaped by two main categories:

- Mandatory reporting: Required by law and enforced by regulations.

- Voluntary reporting: Optional but often expected by

investors, customers, and other stakeholders.

As concerns over Climate Change and environmental sustainability grow, more countries are requiring companies to disclose their sustainability performance, particularly related to climate-related financial risks.

A key framework for this is the Task Force on Climate-related Financial Disclosures (TCFD), which has been integrated into many National regulations.

However, regions like the European Union (EU) have introduced the Corporate Sustainability Reporting Directive (CSRD) with European Sustainability Reporting Standards (ESRS), which go beyond climate-related disclosures to cover broader ESG topics.

Reporting on the SDGs with Double Materiality: To Enhance Corporate Sustainability

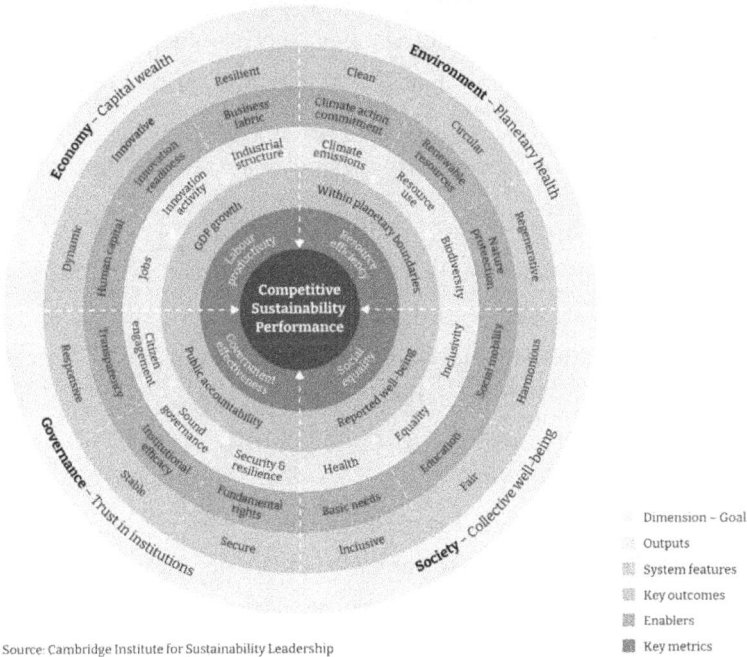

Source: Cambridge Institute for Sustainability Leadership

Despite significant efforts, Global progress on achieving the Sustainable Development Goals (SDGs) remains insufficient. While the SDG targets and indicators were originally designed for countries to measure their progress, the private sector also plays a critical role in driving these goals forward. Without active and strategic engagement from businesses, many SDG targets are unlikely to be met.

Despite the challenge of the SDGs being developed for Member States, they have resonated strongly with the corporate world. According to the Governance & Accountability Institute, Inc. 2023 research on sustainability reporting, 52% of Russell 1000 companies aligned with the SDGs in 2022 – an increase from 32%

in 2019. From the 472 companies aligning with the SDGs, there were 4,170 specific mentions of one or more of the 17 SDGs, with S&P 500 companies making up the majority. This growing commitment is evident across key sectors such as Consumer Staples, Utilities, Real Estate, Materials, and Health Care. However, despite this strong uptake, there are significant challenges in how businesses integrate the SDGs into their reporting practices.

Companies can selectively report on positive contributions to the SDGs while overlooking negative impacts, leading to SDG-washing. Another standard practice in voluntary SDG reporting is that many companies tend to cherry-pick the SDGs that are easier to measure and report on, leading to incomplete and potentially misleading comprehensive assessments on the company's overall SDG performance. Furthermore, there is a significant lack of comprehensive reporting that assesses SDG impacts across the value chain. This selective approach undermines the credibility of SDG-related information and hinders stakeholders from making informed decisions.

A thorough understanding of the context in which they operate, impacts as well as financial risks and opportunities can help companies align their business strategies with Global sustainability priorities. By embedding the SDGs into double materiality assessments, businesses can ensure that their reporting is not only more accurate and credible but also strategically aligned with

long-term business success. Moreover, adopting a double materiality approach can help companies advance strategic action on the SDGs, while also helping to uncover potential risks that could arise from ignoring negative impacts on the SDGs.

To ensure that current SDG reporting practices remain credible, relevant and actionable in a rapidly changing reporting landscape, businesses are urged to report on the SDGs through a double materiality approach. This comprehensive assessment allows businesses to set ambitious, SDG-aligned goals that drive meaningful progress and enhance their resilience and value.

Objectives

- To explore current approaches and practices to integrate SDGs into corporate sustainability reporting processes.

- To equip participants with practical insights that facilitate a deeper integration of the SDGs into sustainability strategy and reporting practices, with a focus on double materiality assessments.

- To engage participants in discussions with reporting experts on the implications of double materiality for SDG reporting.

- To foster a deeper understanding of the interplay between different reporting frameworks, with a focus on the GRI Standards, and how they can be used to drive disclosures on the SDGs.

Navigating ESG Reporting Frameworks: A Guide

As businesses increasingly recognize the importance of Environmental, Social, and Governance (ESG) factors in their operations, selecting the right ESG reporting framework becomes crucial. ESG reporting provides a structured approach to measuring and disclosing a company's sustainability performance and impact. So how to navigate these frameworks and identify the most suitable one for your organization?

1. **Understand Your Objectives:** Begin by clarifying your ESG goals and what you aim to achieve through reporting. Are you looking to enhance transparency, attract socially responsible investors, or align with Global sustainability standards? Knowing your objectives will help you find a framework that aligns with your vision.

2. **Explore Different Frameworks:** There are several popular ESG reporting frameworks available, such as Global Reporting Initiative (GRI), Sustainability Accounting Standards Board (SASB), Task Force on Climate-related Financial Disclosures (TCFD), and United Nations Sustainable Development Goals (SDGs). Each framework focuses on different aspects of ESG, so research their requirements and areas of emphasis.

3. **Industry Relevance:** Consider the nature of your business and industry when selecting a framework. Some frameworks might be more suited to certain sectors, ensuring that your reporting addresses the specific ESG challenges and opportunities relevant to your operations.

4. **Comprehensiveness and Materiality:** Look for a framework that offers comprehensive coverage of ESG topics relevant to your organization. Additionally, prioritize the concept of materiality, which means reporting on issues that significantly impact your business and stakeholders.

5. **Feasibility and Data Availability:** Assess the feasibility of implementing the chosen framework within your organization. Ensure that you have access to the necessary data to report on ESG indicators effectively.

Now, which framework should you adopt? There is no one-size-fits-all answer. The ideal framework for your business depends on various factors, including your industry, geographic location, and stakeholder expectations. Some companies may even choose to combine multiple frameworks for a holistic approach. Which I also recommend.

ESG should start from responsible business conduct and sustainable development (!) Integrating responsible practices into your core business operations fosters a culture of ethical behavior, environmental stewardship, and social responsibility.

Sustainability as a Strategy ™ Framework

Improve your ESG performance and generate quantified triple bottom line results: People, Planet, Profit

This framework is our approach to integrating Sustainability as a Strategy™ at the core of every organization's business model. It is designed to adapt to all industries and sizes and to help organizations find the shortest path to sustainability.

1. **BASELINE**

   Sustainability Maturity Assessment ESG Risks & Opportunities ESG Metrics & KPIs

2. **MATERIALITY**

   Metrics, KPIs & R&Os Prioritization Initiatives Feasibility Study Action Plan & Target Setting

3. **DEPLOYMENT**

   ESG Systems: KPIs Collection & Monitoring ESG Governance & Stakeholders Engagement ESG Initiatives & Performance Improvement

4. COMMUNICATION

ESG Dashboards Outreach Plan (Internal & External) ESG Reporting

5. LEADERSHIP

Influence Industry Peers Cross-Industry Pollination Government Policies Contribution

Embracing ESG Due Diligence: A Path to Sustainable Success

ESG due diligence is not merely a trendy buzzword but a strategic imperative that has become an integral part of decision-making processes for companies of all sizes. It goes beyond short-term profits and focuses on the long-term impact of business operations on our planet, people, and communities. Organizations that embrace ESG due diligence recognize that creating shared value for all stakeholders is the key to sustained growth and resilience.

1. Environmental Responsibility

Addressing environmental challenges is at the forefront of ESG due diligence. Organizations must understand their carbon footprint, resource consumption, and waste generation. By identifying areas where sustainability can be improved, companies can implement eco-friendly practices, adopt renewable energy sources, and reduce their ecological impact. Moreover, integrating climate risks and opportunities into business strategies enhances both operational efficiency and resilience in the face of Climate Change.

2. Social Empowerment

The 'S' in ESG emphasizes the significance of social responsibility. Companies are encouraged to assess their impact on employees, customers, suppliers, and the broader communities they operate in. Ensuring fair labor practices, diversity and inclusion, employee well-being, and responsible sourcing create a positive ripple effect that strengthens social bonds and fosters trust among stakeholders. Empowering people and communities leads to a more engaged and motivated workforce, resulting in increased productivity and innovation.

3. **Governance Excellence**

Effective governance sets the tone for ethical decision-making and transparent business practices. Strong governance structures promote accountability, safeguard against corruption, and uphold the rule of law. By conducting comprehensive ESG due diligence, organizations can identify potential risks related to corporate governance and proactively implement measures to mitigate them. This builds investor confidence, attracts capital, and improves long-term financial performance.

In conclusion, ESG due diligence is not just a compliance exercise but an opportunity to create positive change and forge a sustainable future. It requires collaboration, dedication, and a genuine commitment to making a difference beyond the balance sheet. As professionals, we have the privilege and responsibility to drive this transformative journey and build a more inclusive, resilient, and environmentally conscious business landscape.

Let's take the leap toward ESG excellence and inspire others to join us on this meaningful journey. Together, we can create a better world for generations to come!

Chapter 6

Sustainability Career / Climate Workforce

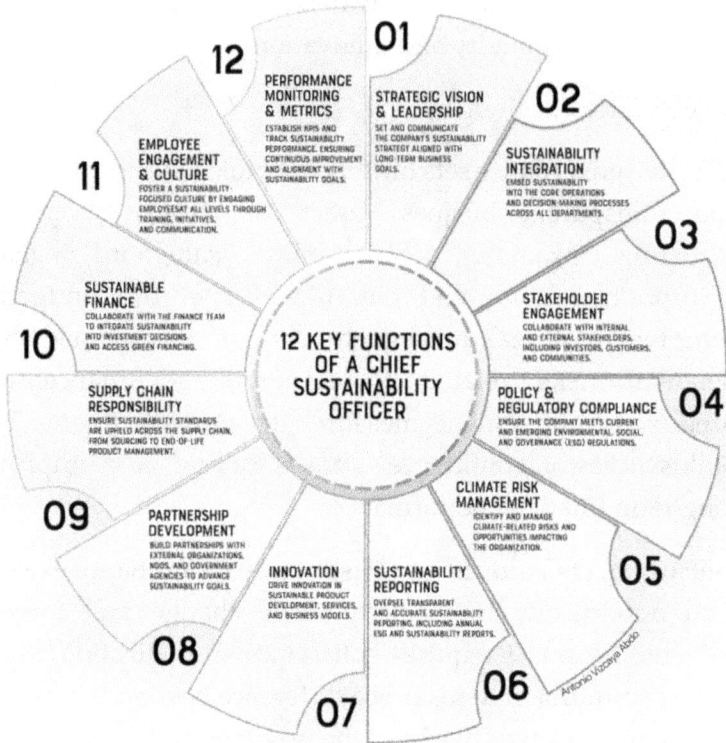

12

01
PERFORMANCE MONITORING & METRICS
ESTABLISH KPIS AND TRACK SUSTAINABILITY PERFORMANCE, ENSURING CONTINUOUS IMPROVEMENT AND ALIGNMENT WITH SUSTAINABILITY GOALS.

STRATEGIC VISION & LEADERSHIP
SET AND COMMUNICATE THE COMPANY'S SUSTAINABILITY STRATEGY ALIGNED WITH LONG-TERM BUSINESS GOALS.

02
SUSTAINABILITY INTEGRATION
EMBED SUSTAINABILITY INTO THE CORE OPERATIONS AND DECISION-MAKING PROCESSES ACROSS ALL DEPARTMENTS.

11
EMPLOYEE ENGAGEMENT & CULTURE
FOSTER A SUSTAINABILITY-FOCUSED CULTURE BY ENGAGING EMPLOYEESAT ALL LEVELS THROUGH TRAINING, INITIATIVES, AND COMMUNICATION.

03
STAKEHOLDER ENGAGEMENT
COLLABORATE WITH INTERNAL AND EXTERNAL STAKEHOLDERS, INCLUDING INVESTORS, CUSTOMERS, AND COMMUNITIES.

10
SUSTAINABLE FINANCE
COLLABORATE WITH THE FINANCE TEAM TO INTEGRATE SUSTAINABILITY INTO INVESTMENT DECISIONS AND ACCESS GREEN FINANCING.

12 KEY FUNCTIONS OF A CHIEF SUSTAINABILITY OFFICER

POLICY & REGULATORY COMPLIANCE
ENSURE THE COMPANY MEETS CURRENT AND EMERGING ENVIRONMENTAL, SOCIAL, AND GOVERNANCE (ESG) REGULATIONS.
04

SUPPLY CHAIN RESPONSIBILITY
ENSURE SUSTAINABILITY STANDARDS ARE UPHELD ACROSS THE SUPPLY CHAIN, FROM SOURCING TO END-OF-LIFE PRODUCT MANAGEMENT.

CLIMATE RISK MANAGEMENT
IDENTIFY AND MANAGE CLIMATE-RELATED RISKS AND OPPORTUNITIES IMPACTING THE ORGANIZATION.

09
PARTNERSHIP DEVELOPMENT
BUILD PARTNERSHIPS WITH EXTERNAL ORGANIZATIONS, NGOS, AND GOVERNMENT AGENCIES TO ADVANCE SUSTAINABILITY GOALS.

05

INNOVATION
DRIVE INNOVATION IN SUSTAINABLE PRODUCT DEVELOPMENT, SERVICES, AND BUSINESS MODELS.

SUSTAINABILITY REPORTING
OVERSEE TRANSPARENT AND ACCURATE SUSTAINABILITY REPORTING, INCLUDING ANNUAL ESG AND SUSTAINABILITY REPORTS.

08

06

07

Antonio Vizcaya Abdo

Develop climate literacy skills for green jobs.

A specially curated track that can address the impact on the Global workforce of reaching net zero, ensuring the next generation is equipped with the skills required to build a sustainable future. Join business chiefs, policymakers and leaders from higher Education institutions across the globe as we tackle how to transform the labour market for a clean-energy future and explore the opportunities and challenges of progressing green skills. Identify emerging best practices for cross-sector collaboration and partnerships to accelerate green skills provision.

More and more individuals in business and wider society realise that we need to reduce greenhouse gas emissions, address Climate Change, and transition to a net zero society. This has led to a demand for climate literacy from managers and employees at all levels, working in organisations across the public, private, and third sector.

Role of business Education in creating a more sustainable, socially responsible future and explore the role of business Education in creating environmental and social sustainability within the framework of specific SDGs. Showcase how cutting-edge, immersive learning technologies can revolutionise business Education and training, making it more accessible than ever before.

Research and innovation towards carbon neutrality and abundant clean energy

The development of energies that carry the potential to meet industrial demands, without exhausting natural resources requires collective action and innovative cross-sector partnerships to ensure carbon neutrality by 2050 and to deliver clean energy that can meet energy security needs.

This track focuses on harnessing research and technological innovations to tackle Global energy challenges, developing the skills necessary for a robust renewable energy workforce and developing policy to deliver a just, sustainable energy transition.

Companies in increasing numbers are pledging a net-zero impact by the middle or end of the century. Fueling this trend are government regulations, stakeholder preferences, and the promise of cost savings and new revenue streams. But many executives have fundamental questions about how to achieve their firm's decarbonization goals.

Net-Zero Transformation guides leaders through sustainability strategy and execution, providing them with tools, concepts, and frameworks to accomplish critical change management across their organizations.

1. Grasp the principles of sustainable practices in various sectors like travel, transportation, buildings, construction, supply chains, and more

2. Understand Global regulatory frameworks for net-zero goals and how they affect your business

3. Evaluate the risks and opportunities associated with implementing a climate pledge for firms in different sectors

4. Learn to leverage tools for carbon measurement and reporting

5. Explore new revenue streams and business models aligned with your net zero objectives.

6. Discover how to lead a strategic transition to sustainability in your organization

7. Learn to leverage tools for carbon measurement and reporting

Chapter 7

People and Planetary Health through Sustainability

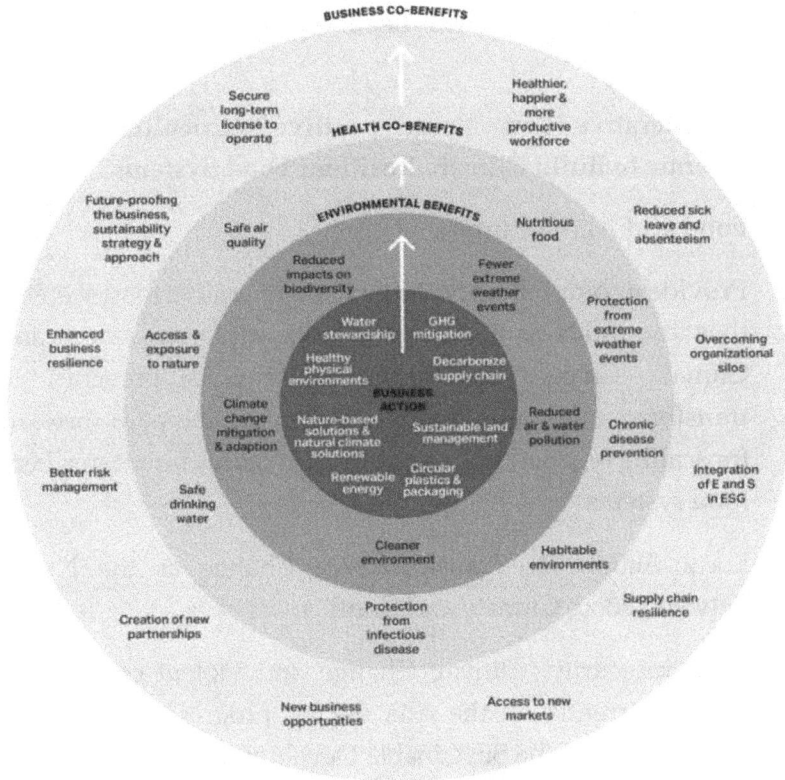

The current wave of human activities is causing substantial changes to our biosphere, upsetting the balance of the planet's natural systems. The climate crisis, Global pollution, biodiversity loss, and changes in land use pose imminent threats to every facet of human health and wellbeing.

The burgeoning planetary emergency carries with it a growing list of health risks. These include an increase in malnutrition, infectious and non-communicable diseases, migration, displacement, conflict, and negative mental health impacts. These risks promise to place a significant burden on health systems, societies, and economies across the globe.

Corporate Governance and Leadership for Environmental Sustainability –

1. **Regenerative and Nature-positive Agriculture as an Avenue to Build Climate Resilient Food Systems.**

   Food and Agriculture

   Provide a comprehensive view of regenerative food systems that can address Global food security, resilience, and Climate Change mitigation. Systemic approaches to transform food value chains and explore the path forward for scaling regenerative agriculture to build climate-resilient food systems.

   Local Action for Transformative Change as the Nexus Between Food, Climate and Conflict.

   Food insecurity, Climate Change and violent conflict are trends currently on the rise, risking progress towards the achievement of the Sustainable Development Goals. There is a well-known link and a vicious cycle between food insecurity and conflict, which is exacerbated by Climate Change. Global efforts and solely top-down initiatives have been failing to address these triple challenges, and there is a growing number of calls for increased local action. Thus, there is a need for better understanding of the role of local initiatives and organizations in contributing to wider systemic change and how they can be combined, or enabled by, Global efforts and stakeholders operating at different scales. what is needed is to foster positive cross-scale interactions and relationships that enable local action for more sustainable and just food systems that are also conflict and climate resilient.

2. Water and Natural Ecosystems

Healthy ecosystems are fundamental for climate regulation. Our planet's marine and terrestrial life absorbs around half of anthropogenic carbon emissions and, when healthy, has a greater potential to mitigate and adapt to Climate Change. Hence, understanding the world's most vulnerable ecosystems is crucial.

Often found in fragile regions, they're disproportionately affected by Climate Change and biodiversity loss, offering early insights into broader ecological shifts. Protecting and restoring these areas benefits local communities and bolsters Global resilience.

Climate Change impacts largely manifest through water. It is the life-giving force on earth, but has far too often been neglected in discussions outside the water sector. Climate Change and human activities have profoundly altered water cycles, affecting aquatic biodiversity, needs and demands for water, sanitation and hygiene (WASH), livelihoods, food production, cities and industry, and human-nature relationships. Showcasing innovative locally-led solutions, amplifying intergenerational indigenous and local voices, and matchmaking collaborations across geographies and sectors to deliver a resilient future.

- Landscapes for water – Scaling up locally-led climate action local communities are on the frontlines of Climate Change impacts, but often they do not have a voice in decision-making that affects them. Showcase best-practices, tools, and local initiatives that strengthen climate action and water resilience, and how they can be upscaled and more systematically incorporated into Global and National processes.

Nature's Wealth: Bridging economic resilience with water and biodiversity prosperity

Here we explore the interconnected relationship between water resilience, biodiversity, and economic stability. We emphasize that water is the linchpin of economic resilience, impacting various sectors such as agriculture, energy, and tourism.

Additionally, the indispensable role of biodiversity and nature in safeguarding our planet's health and human well-being, underscoring the urgency of closing the Global investment gap for their conservation.

Furthermore, the synergy between water and nature, showcasing how healthy ecosystems contribute to clean water resources. Protecting and restoring natural habitats is imperative for enhancing water resilience and mitigating environmental and economic challenges.

- Transformative Leverage and Intervention Points for Climate and Biosphere Resilience.

Earth's resilience hinges on the interplay between climate and the biosphere.

Presently, one-fourth of human carbon emissions are absorbed by land systems, but they're threatened by factors like habitat loss and changing ecosystems. Robust ecosystems better endure climate shifts, securing long-term services like carbon capture. Balancing biosphere conservation with climate goals is vital, yet conflicts arise, potentially harming biodiversity, and undermining conservation goals. Earth's climate results from intricate abiotic, biotic, and societal processes, necessitating systemic thinking. Drivers impacting Global climate and biosphere resilience, lessons from Climate Change mitigation, innovations in understanding climate-biosphere interactions, and their impact on societal shifts for Earth's resilience.

Traditionally, the goal of mitigating greenhouse gas emissions and reducing environmental footprints has spearheaded business action on climate and nature. This goal, critical in managing business impacts and dependencies on nature and climate, continues to be a necessary endeavor. However, there has been a noticeable lack of efforts to align this goal with the health implications of human-induced damage to natural systems.

Recent developments, however, indicate a shift. The intrinsic connection between the health of people and the health of the planet is moving swiftly into the spotlight of the sustainability conversation.

When businesses embrace strategies such as water stewardship, decarbonization of supply chains, sustainable land management, and circular plastics, they are working towards healthier ecosystems and, in turn, healthier communities.

These measures lead to a reduction in environmental impacts and the promotion of cleaner, safer habitats. This domino effect benefits human health by increasing protection from extreme weather events, ensuring safe drinking water, and preventing disease.

Moreover, corporate co-benefits manifest as healthier workforces, reduced absenteeism, resilient supply chains, access to new markets, better risk management, and future-proofing of businesses.

In sum, businesses play a pivotal role in mitigating the planet's health crises and creating a healthier world for its people. As such, the future of sustainability lies in recognizing and reinforcing the interconnection between business actions, planetary health, and human wellbeing.

Sustainability and Decarbonization: Two Sides of the Same Coin

Sustainability focuses on long-term ecosystem health, resource management, and social equity, ensuring that our actions today don't compromise the needs of future generations. It's about more than carbon—it's about fostering an economy that supports people, planet, and profit in harmony.

Decarbonization, on the other hand, focus on reducing greenhouse gas emissions by transitioning to renewable energy, improving energy efficiency, and implementing technologies like carbon capture and storage.

Common between Sustainability and Decarbonization

- Driving innovative technology and research

- Developing resilience and adaptation strategies

- Investing in green infrastructure

- Fostering cross-sector collaboration

- Establishing strong metrics, monitoring, and reporting

Achieving sustainability requires decarbonization, but decarbonization alone is not enough to achieve sustainability. We need an integrated approach.

Support companies on their decarbonization journey, focusing on:

- Emerging technology expertise that includes hydrogen, carbon capture utilization and storage, mobility and renewable fuels

- Decarbonisation services delivering a wide range of climate and decarbonization support, including carbon offsets, circular economy, transition planning, energy efficiency, carbon removal and nature-based solutions

- A climate policy and an incentives dashboard to support clients in understanding the emerging legal regulatory landscape across their geographic and industry footprints

- Prepare clients for the impacts of Climate Change. Provide resources and insights to clients that help shape business models, products and services that address Climate Change and help clients reduce carbon emissions.

Hard Truths for Business Sustainability as We Go into 2025.

1. Climate Change is no longer a distant threat but an immediate strategic risk. Organisations must develop robust and forward-looking risk management frameworks that anticipate and mitigate potential disruptions.

2. Sustainability is not a cost center but an important source of innovation, operational efficiency, and competitive advantage. The most successful enterprises will view ecological constraints as catalysts for breakthrough strategies.

3. Global supply chains must be redesigned with transparency, circularity, and adaptability as core principles. Resilience now trumps pure cost optimisation.

4. Emerging technologies in artificial intelligence and robotics are critical enablers of sustainable transformation. They provide unprecedented capabilities for improving environmental performance.

5. The most competitive organisations will cultivate a workforce that views sustainability as an intrinsic professional competency, not a specialised function.

6. Anticipate increasingly stringent environmental regulations. Proactive compliance is no longer sufficient. Industry leadership requires setting new standards of corporate environmental stewardship.

7. Transparency is the new currency of brand loyalty. Consumers demand verifiable, substantive evidence of sustainability commitments, not superficial marketing narratives.

8. Sustainability challenges cannot be addressed through siloed approaches. Cross-sector collaboration, systems thinking, and holistic problem-solving are essential.

9. Recognise that organisational strategy must operate within scientifically defined planetary ecological boundaries.

Raising Ambitions for Sustainable Development -

How can businesses use the SDGs as a North Star to secure business benefits? Despite increasing business engagement and stakeholder demand for action on the SDGs, many companies still feel overwhelmed and uncertain about how the Goals can be applied to their business. This Volume will explore how companies can secure business benefits by supporting measurable, credible, and ambitious targets to attain the SDGs by 2030. will share insights on how businesses can identify which SDGs are most relevant to stakeholders, establish metrics and business processes to future-proof your business, and how you can collaborate with business, government, and civil society partners to advance the Goals – and secure business benefits.

ESG as a Lever for Creating Sustainable Businesses

An increasing number of investors have begun to use environmental, social, and governance (ESG) performance criteria to determine how to allocate their investments. Using ESG allows investors to assess the effect businesses are having on society and the environment, and to hold them accountable to the claims they are making about their effect on society and the environment. Presumably, the adoption of new and better business models will result from businesses hoping to receive a high ESG rating. So far, though, ESG investing is more vision than practice; it lacks the universally accepted definitions and reporting guidelines that would leave to better governance and accountability. Rather than abandon ESG, attention should be paid to how to effectively turn it into a lever that will entice businesses to perform better.

ESG Standards, Frameworks, and Ranking

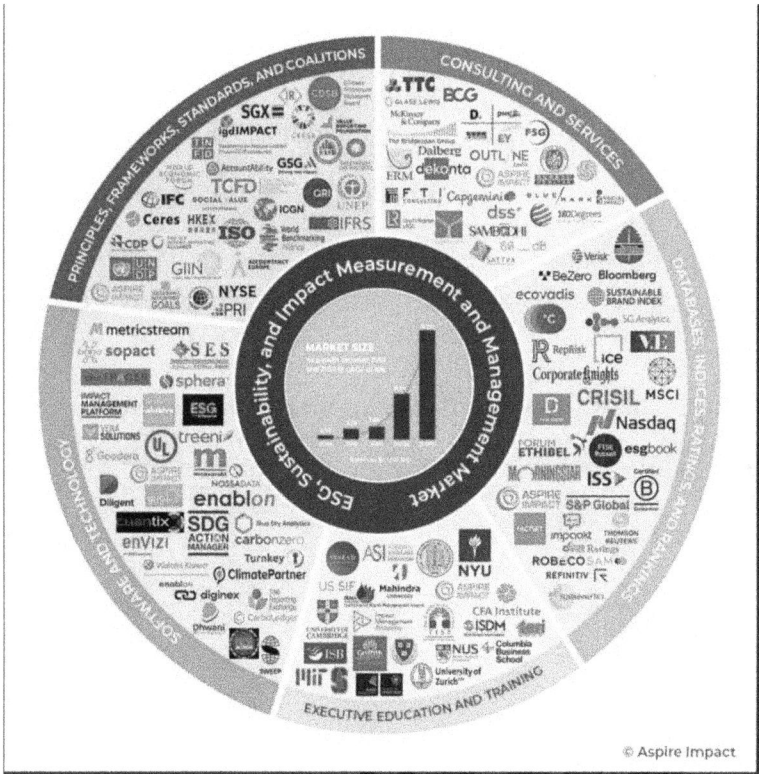

© Aspire Impact

As the world shifts towards a more sustainable future, Environmental, Social, and Governance (ESG) considerations are becoming increasingly important for businesses. But with various ESG standards and frameworks available, it can be challenging to navigate and understand which ones to adopt.

Here's a brief overview:

- ✓ ESG standards and regulations are guidelines and laws used to evaluate a company's environmental, societal, and governance factors.

- ✓ There is currently no single Global ESG standard framework, but several independent frameworks can help businesses develop their ESG strategy and policies, such as:

- ✓ The Global Reporting Initiative

- ✓ The Sustainability Accounting Standards Board (SASB)

- ✓ The United Nations Sustainable Development Goals (SDGs)

ESG ranking systems, such as MSCI ESG, Sustainalytics, and CDP, assess a company's ESG performance and provide a score or rating.

To ensure a comprehensive ESG approach, businesses should:

1. Identify and engage relevant stakeholders

2. Set clear KPIs and goals

3. Prepare for change and crisis management

4. Train employees and ensure role-specific responsibilities

5. Outline policy execution strategies

6. Monitor and enforce compliance

7. Review and adjust policies regularly

By adopting ESG standards and frameworks, businesses can:

- ✓ Improve regulatory compliance

- ✓ Enhance risk management

✓ Demonstrate commitment to stakeholders

✓ Gain a competitive edge

✓ Achieve cost savings

Let's work together to create a more sustainable future.

Chapter 8

Building ESG: A Look at Industry-Specific Risks & Mitigations

Environmental, Social, and Governance (ESG) factors are increasingly influencing business decisions across various industries. As stakeholders, investors, and consumers demand greater transparency and accountability, companies are facing growing pressure to address ESG risks.

Key Risks:

1. Manufacturing Sector:

   - Risks: High emissions, waste generation, resource depletion, worker safety.

   - Mitigation: Invest in renewable energy, circular economy practices, and robust employee safety programs.

2. Construction Sector:

   - Risks: Soil erosion, resource consumption, worker safety, community impact.

   - Mitigation: Implement sustainable building practices, prioritize worker training, and engage with local communities.

3. Hospitality Sector:

   - Risks: High energy/water usage, waste generation, data privacy, fair labor practices.

   - Mitigation: Optimize energy/water efficiency, reduce

waste, implement strong data security measures, and ensure fair wages and benefits.

4. Energy, Oil, & Gas Sector:

- Risks: Environmental damage, resource depletion, indigenous displacement, employee health.

- Mitigation: Invest in renewable energy sources, prioritize safety and environmental protection, and engage with local communities.

5. Mobile Telecoms Sector:

- Risks: E-waste, energy usage, data privacy, digital divide.

- Mitigation: Implement e-waste recycling programs, optimize energy consumption, strengthen data security, and promote digital inclusion.

6. Packaging Sector:

- Risks: Plastic waste, environmental harm, supplier pressure, dangerous packaging.

- Mitigation: Invest in sustainable packaging solutions, ensure supply chain transparency, and prioritize product safety.

7. Pharmaceuticals Sector:

- Risks: Water pollution, waste disposal, access affordability, drug misuse.

- Mitigation: Implement waste reduction strategies, ensure affordable access to medication, and address drug misuse through Education and support programs.

8. Agriculture Sector:

- Risks: Pesticide pollution, water scarcity, land degradation, animal welfare.

- Mitigation: Promote sustainable farming practices, conserve water resources, and prioritize animal welfare.

How is Your Industry Adapting to the Evolving ESG Landscape?

INDUSTRY-SPECIFIC ESG RISKS   ⓒ Certainty

	RISK		
INDUSTRY	ENVIRONMENT	SOCIAL	GOVERNANCE
Manufacturing	• Waste • Emissions • Pollutants • Energy / resource usage	• Stakeholder health • Supplier pressure • Exploitation	• Financial transparency • Board diversity • Executive compensation
Construction	• Deforestation • Soil erosion • Natural resource requirements	• Worker wellbeing • Low wages • Noise, traffic, waste production	• Regulations (OSHA) • Subcontractor relationships • Project oversight
Hospitality	• Energy & water usage • GHG emissions • Waste pollution	• Customer privacy • Diversity • Working conditions	• Fair pricing • Appropriate marketing • Open accounting
Energy, Oil, & Gas	• Ecosystem impact • Resource usage • Habitat damage	• Indigenous displacement • Employee health risks • Land loss	• Emissions reporting • Ethical decision-making
Mobile Telecoms	• E-waste • Energy usage • GHG emissions	• Data privacy • Social isolation • Digital gap	• Ethical marketing • Open accounting • Telecom legislation
Packaging	• Plastic trash • Climate change • Environmental harm	• Labor health risk • Inadequate pay • Supplier pressure • Dangerous packaging	• Transparent labeling • Accurate product information • Ethical marketing
Pharmaceuticals	• Water pollution • Improper waste disposal • Resource depletion	• Antibiotic resistance • Access • Affordability • Drug misuse	• Reporting • Moral decision-making • Drug regulatory compliance
Agriculture	• Water scarcity • Pesticide pollution • Natural capital depletion	• Consumer health • Land grabs • Displacement • Worker health & compensation	• Moral land management • Animal care • Land usage

How to Write a Sustainability Statement: Complete Checklist

Crafting a Sustainability Reporting Standards (SRS)-sustainability statement requires meticulous attention to data accuracy and narrative consistency. This checklist will guide you step-by-step through the process to enable compliance and the creation of a compelling, data-driven report.

1. **Align with the Management Report**

   - Link to your corporate strategy: Investors and analysts will integrate your SRS data points into their valuation models. Ensure that each data point aligns with your corporate strategy and equity story.

   - Maintain a consistent narrative: Approach sustainability reporting with the same precision as financial reporting. Tie each sustainability claim back to your overall business strategy and operating context.

   - Example: If your emissions have increased year-on-year, explain this in the context of expanding operations, but also highlight your long-term decarbonization strategy.

2. **Conduct a Double Materiality Assessment (DMA)**

   - Identify key sustainability matters: Start with a broad range of topics, then screen them based on their relevance to your industry, focusing on both "impact" and "financial" perspectives.

   - Prioritize material topics: After your screening process, focus on topics that have significant ESG impacts, risks or opportunities.

3. Organise Data Point Disclosures

- Data-point-by-data-point approach: Each disclosure must specifically address relevant ESRS data points. This approach enables compliance and makes your report easier to analyze for investors and financial analysts.

- Link impacts to business strategy: Provide a narrative about how your environmental or social impacts affect your business model.

- Example: If your workforce training is a key part of decarbonizing your operations, ensure the data connects to operating new technology and delivering on decarbonization goals. You can align this process using our Plan & Strategize solution.

4. Use Appendices Effectively

- Include detailed tables: Use an appendix to present your SRS content index and the datapoint table. This keeps the main narrative clean while offering in-depth details for analysts.

- Include data below materiality thresholds: For data that is no longer material but still requested by investors or ratings agencies, place it in the appendix of the sustainability statement for transparency.

5. Ensure Faithful Representation

- Meet SRS qualitative characteristics: Your data must be faithfully represented, ensuring it is complete, neutral and accurate. It must also be relevant, understandable, verifiable, and comparable across reporting periods and with other companies in your industry.

- Avoid selective disclosure: Clearly state all material topics, and explain any that you deem non-material to avoid potential issues with auditors or analysts.

- Example: If biodiversity is not material to your operations, provide a justification, particularly if it's a concern in your industry. For better management of your supply chain impacts, consider our Supplier Assessment solution.

6. **Structure Your Sustainability Statement**

- Four key sections: Organize your report according to the ESRS structure, including general information, environmental data, social aspects, and governance details.

- Utilise a wireframe: Ensure that your report's structure is compliant with ESRS guidelines while maintaining readability and a logical flow of information.

- Provide narrative support: Strengthen your data disclosures by linking each point back to your business model and strategy.

7. **Prepare for Audit**

- Conduct pre-audit checks: Ensure that all material data points have been disclosed and properly tracked, and verify phase-in options taken, if any.

- Verify completeness: Use dashboards or tools to track your progress, ensuring all disclosures have been addressed. This is where visualizations can come in handy, as they allow you to get a general overview of your entire progress.

Final Thoughts

Writing a comprehensive SRS sustainability statement requires balancing technical compliance with narrative clarity. This checklist will guide you through the key steps to ensure that your report is both compliant and insightful.

Leveraging Finance for the Global Goals

As Climate Change upends the lives of millions and degrades the natural environment across the world, the finance sector has a vital role to play in enabling societies to respond these social and environmental challenges. The finance sector in Business Companies will have to

1. Provide essential capital for climate adaptation and mitigation measures

2. Exert positive influence on both public and private actors, serving as an example

3. Support governments in building more sustainable and environmentally friendly economies

As Sustainability becomes a priority for businesses, the Chief Sustainability Officer plays a central role in driving strategy and implementation. Here are 12 key functions that outline the responsibilities of this position:

Strategic Vision & Leadership – Aligning sustainability goals with long-term business objectives.

1. Sustainability Integration – Incorporating sustainability into core operations and decision-making across all departments.

2. Stakeholder Engagement – Engaging with internal and

external stakeholders, including investors, customers, and communities.

3. Policy & Regulatory Compliance – Ensuring adherence to current and emerging ESG regulations.

4. Climate Risk Management – Identifying and managing climate-related risks and opportunities.

5. Sustainability Reporting – Overseeing accurate and transparent ESG reporting.

6. Innovation – Leading innovation in sustainable product development and business models.

7. Partnership Development – Establishing partnerships with NGOs, external organizations, and government bodies.

8. Supply Chain Responsibility – Applying sustainability standards throughout the supply chain.

9. Sustainable Finance – Working with finance teams to integrate sustainability into investment decisions.

10. Employee Engagement & Culture – Building a sustainability-focused culture through training and communication.

11. Performance Monitoring & Metrics – Establishing KPIs and tracking sustainability performance.

The CSO role is crucial in embedding sustainability into the business model, ensuring alignment with strategic goals and regulatory standards.

Principles of Finance in the Sustainability Journey

Welcome to the sustainability journey in finance. The journey consists of four steps. We start with the why question, why does sustainability matter?

This step discusses the sustainability challenges we are all facing. Next, we discuss the what question of sustainability. Sustainability is about the transition of companies from unsustainable to sustainable production practices.

Then we move to finance, how can investors and bankers finance sustainable companies?

Finally, we need to stay the transition to sustainable, corporate, and financial world. The key message is that we move from maximizing profit or financial value only to integrated value, which combines financial, social, and environmental value. In other words, we include the impact of companies on the society and on the earth system in our calculations.

Back to Our Sustainability Journey

The first step is about the sustainability challenges, both on the social front, think about hunger, poor healthcare, child labor, underpayment, gender equality. And on the environmental front, Climate Change, loss of biodiversity, shortages of fresh water.

The United Nations has developed a Global strategy to tackle these challenges, the Sustainable Development Goals, in shorthand, the SDGs. These goals should be met by 2030. It's good to realize that these goals can have an impact on the Global level, think about Global warming due to Climate Change, but also at the local level. The key word here is bioregion, which emphasizes local populations, knowledge, and solutions for the social and environmental challenges at the bioregion level. The second step is about the real world of companies, where production takes place and services are delivered.

The social and environmental problems are linked to the production process, think about pollution, working conditions. How can we steer companies towards sustainable business practices?

There is a role, of course, for government to set regulations and taxation, an example is a carbon tax to reduce carbon emissions. But there's also a role for companies themselves to behave properly. That's the field of corporate governance, either added shareholders in charge or a broader set of stakeholders. Next to shareholders, also employees, customers, the wider society, and Earth system.

In the second step, we start with the purpose or mission of companies. What do they really want to achieve? We then move on to strategies and business models. And finish with integrated reporting, where companies show their impact on financial, social, and natural capitals. Only in the third step, we come across finance. How can financial institutions allocate funds to sustainable companies? These financial institutions include investment funds, such as Pension funds or large asset managers, banks, and insurance companies. For investors, the question is to move from investing for short-term profits to long-term value creation. That means, shifting from buying and selling stocks on a daily basis to long-term investment. Committed shareholders engage with companies in good social and environmental practices. The same is relevant for banks, new forms of lending for sustainable and circular businesses.

Finally, insurance companies manage long-term risk. First, insurers want to reduce the risk of hurricanes and floodings, that's what we call prevention. Next, insurers have to provide cover for this bad weather conditions when they happen.

The fourth step is transition. Business as usual is no longer possible. Companies that don't adapt or transition to the new sustainable economy face extinction, they don't survive. That makes the business case for sustainable finance very clear, to invest or lend on a viable and profitable basis. Financial institutions should focus on companies that are prepared or are preparing for sustainable predictions. These companies may be around in the future, the companies that don't change will not be around. An example is Kodak, which did not prepare for digital photographing and is now a faltering company. Preparing for a transition requires a change of mindset in the corporate and financial world. This course helps out with integrated thinking to find new pathways and tools and leaving behind all practices. Welcome to the world of transition dynamics. The upper part of old practices will die out, while the new emerging practices are coming from the bottom. I invite you to be part of these emerging practices, creating a new sustainable world.

The world faces several sustainability challenges. The aim is to keep the planet livable for current and future generations of people. Let's start with the environment. Human activities are increasingly affecting the Earth's ecosystems and threaten our own ability to live on the planet. The framework of planetary boundaries defines a safe operating space for humanity. Planetary boundaries define the ecological capacity of Earth. That is, the ability of Earth's ecosystems to maintain their condition and to produce goods and services that we humans use. The green zone in the picture is the safe operating space. Yellow represents the zone of uncertainty with increasing risk. Red indicates the zone of high risk. It's an issue of potential harm, and we don't have all the scientific knowledge about this. So, we use a strategy called the precautionary principle.

The planetary boundary is at the intersection of the green zone and the yellow zone, where the safe operating zone meets the uncertainty zone. Let's look at the control variable for Climate Change. At this rate, we will cross into the red zone of high risk in 12 or 13 years. The upper limit of the yellow zone is 450 parts per million. If we stay within this limit, then we have a fair chance of limiting Global warming to two degrees Celsius. This is the intersection of the yellow and red zones. Now let's look at another variable, changes in land systems. Were already on the yellow zone there too. We use the amount of force to plan as a control variable for land systems because forests play an important role in controlling the linked dynamics of land use and climate.

We measure the amount of forested land now compared to the amount of forested land before humans started to use it or change it. The planetary boundary is at 75 percent forest on the planet. We currently have 62 percent forest, and that amount is dwindling. But we are not only in the yellow zone, we're in the red zone for the loss of biodiversity and for the use of freshwater.

Water shortages are already common in some places around the equator. Except these environmental threats, there are also substantial threats to the world's social order. Human rights assert everyone's fundamental moral claim to life's essentials. We should all be entitled to food, water, health care, Education, freedom of expression, political participation, and personal security. But many people are still living below the proposed norm.

Professor Kate Raworth, a British economist and author, summarize the social foundations and planetary boundaries in her 2017 book, Doughnut Economics: Seven Ways to Think. Like a 21st Century Economist. In her book, she shows how the safe and fair space for humanity lies between this social foundation of human well-being and the ecological ceiling of planetary pressure.

Sustainable development combines the concept of planetary boundaries with a complementary concept of social foundations.

If Sustainable development were adopted worldwide, it would mean that current and future generations of people would have the resources they need. They would have food, clean water, health care, and a source of energy, all without putting stress on planet Earth's systems. There's a Global plan for this. There are 17 Sustainable Development Goals formulated by the United Nations.

SDGs are the Global strategy for sustainable development. They can be considered wicked problems. This means that there are no quick wins, no easy solutions available, and that we can only strive for the most optimal approach towards a solution in partnership with other stakeholders. Only if we work together, we have a chance of ending hunger, poverty, or inequality. This model developed by Carl Folke and his team from the Stockholm Resilience Center, clusters the SDGs in four layers, the biosphere, society, economy, and partnerships.

Without a stable biosphere is hard to build a functioning society, and without a stable society, how can you build an economy that works for all? Partnerships are crucial in making everything happen. When you design a business model, you have to take these elements into account as well. The future is not so much about money anymore, it is about value creation, financial value of course, but also social value and ecological value. How to organize your business in such a way that it delivers multiple values will be a key question, difficult to answer, but also an exciting challenge for adventurers' minds. As the current world is mostly cast in money terms, for companies we talk about profit, and for governments we talk about GDP. The SDG agenda means that we need to transition from business as usual to sustainable business models that use sustainable finance. Is your business model future-proof in this new world of sustainable development?

FINANCE as a Powerful Tool for SDGs

An important role of finance is to allocate funding to its most productive use and to stimulate value creation. Finance can steer investments to sustainable companies and projects without sacrificing financial return and speed up the transition to a sustainable economy. In this way, finance can be a powerful force for positive change, but how is it possible? You may ask, as finance's always thought of as looking for the highest financial return in the short or even shortest term. While sustainable development is all about creating value in the long-term, companies play an important role in achieving the Sustainable Development Goals through long-term value creation. So how can companies steer their business towards sustainable practices in a transition?

This question touches upon the fundamental question of corporate finance. What is the objective of the corporation? For decades, maximizing profits has been the leading objective in corporate finance which boils down to maximizing shareholder or financial value, but often a shareholder model is holding company back from sustainable business practices.

An alternative approach is to broaden the objective of the company to optimizing the total or integrated value in the long-term. Long-term value creation; this approach combines optimizing the financial, social and natural capitals. In that way, the interests of stakeholders are ranked equally important. The shift from the old shareholder model to the new stakeholder model requires new rules for corporate governance and decision-making on corporate investments to deal with the different interests. It basically means incorporating the social and environmental dimensions.

Now we get to the one-million-dollar question. The old view is that taking social and environmental concerns into account will cost investors money. The financial return will just be lower. A new emerging view is that there is no need to sacrifice return when investing in solutions for sustainable development. To put it even stronger, investors should invest in the future to preserve the value of their investments. The underlying premise is that social and environmental standards are tightened over time that could be caused through regulation and taxes, such as carbon taxes. It could also be caused through reputation effects, such as campaigns by NGOs or consumers avoiding wrong products. Let me give you an example. Coal will not be used anymore when carbon taxes are introduced over time. Another example; underpayment in developing countries will disappear as these countries tighten their social legislation.

These examples of the transition from unsustainable to sustainable business practices. Finance is about anticipating such changes. From a risk perspective, financial institutions have already started to avoid financing companies with unsustainable business models built for example on fossil fuels or cheap labor because these are expected to be unprofitable investments in the future. Fossil fuel companies are thought of as becoming stranded assets when future carbon taxes or improved technology moves the business case to renewable energy. The reduced cost of solar energy and wind parks is already shifting the playing field of investments in the energy sector. It gets more exciting when we switch from a risk perspective to the opportunity perspective. Some advanced investors look for companies that provide solutions for fresh water, healthcare, renewable energy and land restoration. These investors tend to look beyond financial markets which only convey financial information. They collect fundamental analysis of a company's business model to uncover the social and environmental value next to the financial value.

By doing a broad analysis offering the financial, social and environmental dimensions, investors aim to select the companies of the future. Companies that do well in the future will also provide an appropriate financial return. The financial sector can do well by doing good. Finance plays thus an important role in achieving the Sustainable Development Goals. Sustainable finance can for example, speedup the availability of renewable energy, clean water, and healthcare for all.

What is Sustainability Data?

Sustainability data focuses on resource utilization, including how much energy, water, materials, and waste are you using or generating, how much time you are allocating to your efforts, and how much money you are saving or spending on those efforts.

Why do We Need to Collect Data?

By collecting and analyzing data on a wide range of sustainability-related factors – including energy and resource use, greenhouse gas emissions, and supply chain performance – companies will generate the deep insights they need to guide their sustainability-related initiatives and improve their resource efficiency. Using the latest tools and techniques, hospitals are now conducting real-time (or near real-time) sustainability analysis on vast quantities of data for the past, present, and future.

Measurement is one of the keys to management, and data can empower leaders to make decisions based on facts, trends, and statistics.

With so much information out there, CSO can make the best decisions about sustainability program strategy and success. Collecting and understanding data about how your organization operates leads to knowledge that will help you improve decision-making, refine goals, and focus efforts.

"I believe that the data will set you free. At the end of the day, it's about how you turn those pieces of information into insights that will improve business."

Data collection and Sustainability analytics help organizations understand the cost, impact, and performance of their past and present sustainability initiatives and anticipate future conditions and requirements, allowing them to unlock hidden value and build more resilient enterprises.

Accelerating business action on Climate Change adaptation with the impacts of Climate Change becoming more frequent and intense, the need for businesses to manage these risks and understand the opportunities for collaboration has never been more important.

Climate Mitigation — the reduction or prevention of greenhouse gas emissions — has been a key focus for businesses in addressing Climate Change, planning for climate adaptation — efforts to reduce the negative impacts of Climate Change and leverage the opportunities — remains a challenge for many.

Climate Change adaptation is a business imperative to avoid economic losses resulting from Climate Change; to innovate new ways to create revenue growth, cost savings and sustainability; and to protect local communities and ecosystems where companies operate.

Businesses can use to develop their approach to climate adaptation strategy using the below framework-

- Enhance resilience: Assess the impacts of climate risks on business and act to adapt and build resilience, especially by working with suppliers and communities connected to the value chain to enhance business resilience.

- Capitalise on opportunities: Leverage products, services and business models that help businesses, communities and ecosystems adapt and build resilience while also pursuing adaptation opportunities that contribute to efficiency, sustainability and Climate Change mitigation.

- Shape collaborative outcomes: Participate in multi-stakeholder efforts that promote action on Climate Change adaptation and deliver transformative projects to build community and ecosystem resilience.

- Discuss the role that stakeholders across sectors can play in building resilience for communities, countries, and companies.

- What are effective adaptation measures? What are benefits from adaptation, and how can they improve economic and financial outcomes?

- How have organizations successfully aligned stakeholders to take action to adapt?

- How can adaptation best be financed?

As we look ahead, the SDGs are not just a framework for global development—they are a blueprint for resilient, purpose-driven business. In a world shaped by complexity, uncertainty, and urgency, companies that align profit with progress will not only lead markets, but help redefine them. The path forward demands more than compliance; it calls for leadership, innovation, and deep collaboration across sectors and borders. Businesses that embrace this challenge won't just survive the decade ahead—they will shape a future where inclusive growth, planetary health, and human dignity are not ideals, but outcomes. The time to act is now—and the choice to lead is yours.

References

https://www.stockholmresilience.org/research/planetary-boundaries.

https://sdgs.un.org/goals

https://www.bcg.com/capabilities/social-impact/expert-insights

https://www.pwc.com/gx/en/services/sustainability/public ations/critical-business-actions-for-clim ate-change-adaptation.html

https://www3.weforum.org/docs/WEF_The_Chairpesons_G uide2023.pdf

https://lnkd.in/dh6PUhDi

www.bcg.com

plana.earth

competentboards.com

www.coursera.org

gbc-Education.org

blogs.microsoft.com

www.ga-institute.com

iucn.org

leadthechange.bard.edu

fr.coursera.org

remplatestst.ilo.org

theelders.org

www.ingramcontent.com/pod-product-compliance
Lightning Source LLC
Chambersburg PA
CBHW061024220326
41597CB00019BB/3389